D0389257

San Diego Christian College
2100 Greenfield Drive
El Cajon, CA 92019

THE LEADERSHIP LIBRARY
VOLUME 19
SINS OF THE BODY

Other books in THE LEADERSHIP LIBRARY

Well-Intentioned Dragons by Marshall Shelley

Liberating the Leader's Prayer Life by Terry Muck

Clergy Couples in Crisis by Dean Merrill

When It's Time to Move by Paul D. Robbins, ed.

Learning to Lead by Fred Smith

What Every Pastor Needs to Know about Music, Youth, and Education
   by Garth Bolinder, Tom McKee, and John Cionca

Helping Those Who Don't Want Help by Marshall Shelley

Preaching to Convince by James D. Berkley, ed.

When to Take a Risk by Terry Muck

Weddings, Funerals, and Special Events
   by Eugene Peterson, Calvin Miller, and others

Making the Most of Mistakes by James D. Berkley

Leaders by Harold Myra, ed.

Being Holy, Being Human by Jay Kesler

Secrets of Staying Power by Kevin A. Miller

The Magnetic Fellowship by Larry K. Weeden, ed.

The Healthy Hectic Home by Marshall Shelley

The Contemplative Pastor by Eugene H. Peterson

Called into Crisis by James D. Berkley

253.2
M942sb

THE LEADERSHIP LIBRARY

Volume

19

Sins of the Body

(Benguiat)

Ministry in a Sexual Society

Terry Muck, ed.

Carol Stream, Illinois

WORD PUBLISHING

Dallas · London · Sydney · Singapore

SINS OF THE BODY

© 1989 Christianity Today, Inc.

A LEADERSHIP/Word Book. Copublished by Christianity Today, Inc. and Word, Inc. Distributed by Word Books.

Cover art by Paul Turnbaugh

All rights reserved. Except for brief quotations in reviews, no part of this book may be reproduced in any form or transmitted in any form or by any means, electronic or mechanical, including photocopy, recording, or any information storage and retrieval system, without written permission from the publisher.

Library of Congress Cataloging-in-Publication Data

Sins of the body: ministry in a sexual society / Terry C. Muck, ed.
    p. cm. — (The Leadership Library : v. 19)
        ISBN 0-917463-24-2 : $10.95
        1. Clergy—Sexual behavior.   2. Sex—Religious aspects—
    Christianity.   3. Pastoral counseling.   I. Muck, Terry C., 1947- .
    II. Series.
BV4392.S56 1989   89-9765
253′.2—dc20   CIP

9801239 AGF 987654321

Printed in the United States of America

CONTENTS

INTRODUCTION

Pastors are tempted sexually.

The words are not pleasant to write. Stripped of all pretense and posturing, such a statement seems almost too bald, too frank. Even though in our heart of hearts we would probably agree to the *truth* of the statement, we still cringe at saying it without any euphemisms to soften the verbal blow.

But that's just the point. Part of the reason sexual temptation is such a profound problem for ministers is few have been willing to say so. Some even deny it is true. Most, however, try to soften the blow with qualifying statements and verbal dodges. This reluctance to talk about the problem can be traced to several roots.

Root one: we are invested with a holy calling. To admit to sexual temptation in the same breath as we mention our holy office is tantamount, some seem to think, to admitting defeat in our life's work.

Root two: we are called to help solve the problems of other people's sexual temptations. To admit to the same problems, some think, will make us less effective counselors. Thus we are left stewing in our own sexual juices — unable to admit our own weakness, titillated by others' descriptions of their weaknesses, sometimes even pursued by those same people who come to us for help. Ministry is difficult.

Root three is the seamier side. Consider the following names: Jim Bakker, Jessica Hahn, Jimmy Swaggart. When we think of sex and ministers, events of the recent years force us to think of these names. Yet it's an unfair association. High-profile televangelists and local church leaders have little in common. The intentional, willful sexual escapades of the rich and famous are not the usual stuff of local church ministry. For most of us, sexual temptation is the unconscious background static of everyday living, not the stereophonic soap opera of hotel trysts and red-light liaisons. In its own way, local church sexual temptation is every bit as powerful and dangerous. But the dynamics are very different.

Still, the association is there. And to mention that we are tempted sexually — to anyone, whether wife, counselor, friend, or colleague — is to throw ourselves into unsavory company in the minds of most.

Is there nowhere a sympathetic — or better yet, helpful — ear?

In LEADERSHIP Journal over the years we have tried to provide a sympathetic and helpful resource on several fronts. For one, we have encouraged local church leaders to speak frankly on our pages about sexual temptation. Some courageous leaders have taken us up on this opportunity. They have told their stories and struggles.

This has raised questions in the minds of some. Should we be so candid about the problem of sexual temptation? Are we wise to encourage open talk about so dangerous a problem? We recognized the danger, but after much prayer and counsel, we have taken the position that talking about a serious problem is better than not talking about it. Judging from our readers' overwhelming responses, we think we chose the right course.

But to safeguard against the dangers, we attacked the problem on another front. We took steps to put the problem in realistic perspective. We wanted to avoid whitewashing a serious problem. But we also wanted to avoid the opposite danger: sensationalizing a few random incidents.

Thus, LEADERSHIP Journal commissioned a poll to determine the scope of the problem. The research department of Christianity Today, Inc., mailed nearly one thousand surveys to pastors, and 30 percent responded.

According to the results of this survey, sexual temptation among pastors is indeed a serious problem—70 percent of the respondents expressed the belief that pastors are particularly vulnerable.

In the words of one respondent: "This is, by far, the greatest problem I deal with."

We found out many other things, sobering things, about the scope of the problem.

The Struggle

The survey probed the frequency of behavior that pastors themselves feel is inappropriate.

Since you've been in local church ministry, have you ever done anything with someone (not your spouse) that you feel was sexually inappropriate? The responses: 23 percent yes; 77 percent no. The "inappropriate" behavior was left undefined—possibly ranging from unguarded words to flirtation to adultery. Subsequent questions were more specific.

Have you ever had sexual intercourse with someone other than your spouse since you've been in local-church ministry? Yes: 12 percent. No: 88 percent. And of that 88 percent, many indicated their purity had not come easily.

"I don't believe any of us, especially emotionally charged preachers, are chaste by design nearly as much as by the grace of God," wrote one respondent. "Numbers of times, only God has prevented me from acting out my designs in this area."

To lend some perspective to these figures, CTi researchers also surveyed almost one thousand subscribers of *Christianity Today* magazine who are *not* pastors. Incidences of immorality were nearly double: 45 percent indicated having done something they considered sexually inappropriate and 23 percent said they had had extramarital intercourse.

Pastors were also asked about the major factors that led them to this relationship. The most frequent answer: "Physical and emotional attraction" (78 percent). "Marital dissatisfaction" was a distant second (41 percent).

Among professional counselors and those who work with pastors, these figures were cause for both concern and relief.

Gary Collins, a professor of counseling at Trinity Evangelical Divinity School, was concerned that those entering the ministry "know the biblical, theological world, but they don't know the real world in which we live. We're living in a Corinthian age, but we're preparing students for the Victorian age."

His words mirror a statement by a pastor answering the survey who acknowledged having had extra-marital sexual contact and who wrote, "When I was a younger pastor, I did not take the temptation seriously. Only after I fell into it once did I become aware."

On the other hand, David Mace, a counselor who, with his wife, Vera, has written several books on marriage, including *What's Happening to Clergy Marriages*, said that if the survey findings held any surprise for him, it was "that the proportions are so small, that for every pastor who has slipped on this icy surface, there are so many who have kept their balance."

But Gary Collins wondered about some of the internal and intangible consequences of inappropriate sexual behavior: "What are these people doing with the guilt and the fear that they'll be found out?" Such fear, he said, tends to push pastors toward one of two extremes. "It either makes them tentative, holding back even from healthy involvement with other people, or it leads them to preach strongly against sexual sin so the congregation won't suspect what they've done."

Where to Turn

Is there any help available for pastors suffering from sexual temptations? When asked whether they have close friends or family members with whom they are able to discuss sexual temptations, 57 percent said yes, 43 percent no.

"We have *no one* to turn to," wrote one pastor. "We are afraid to go to a counselor for fear that word of our problems will somehow leak out."

Wrote another: "I wouldn't dare tell a fellow minister my problems in this area. My denomination would forgive murder, but not impurity of thought!"

Pastors were divided on whether to disclose temptations to their spouses. *If married, do you talk to your spouse about the sexual temptations you feel?* Fifty-one percent said yes; 49 percent said rarely or never.

Psychologist Larry Crabb was concerned that pastors aren't allowed to admit their vulnerability: "It's rare for a pastor to feel comfortable as anything other than a model Christian. Most churches require their pastors to live in denial."

One pastor, when asked what resources pastors have for resisting temptation, wrote simply, "Few to none." The survey responses indicated that pastors feel a fuller, more open discussion of the subject is needed.

Describing the attitude in their homes as they were raised, 76 percent said "sex was never talked about." Yet as one pastor said, "We need to be talking about sex. The school does and people on the street do and TV does, but Christians don't. Address the issue! Just don't tell me to act like I don't feel these things."

In response to this request for help (and our belief that discussion will help) on the troublesome topic of sexual temptation, the chapters in this book are an attempt to address some of the tough questions.

The first part of the book deals with personal sexual temptation. The second part details ways to protect ourselves from situations that frequently lead to pastoral indiscretions. The third part takes a look at how to help those around us who suffer from various sexual problems—without getting embroiled ourselves. The final section is a note of grace: there is hope, there are ways out.

The topics, at times, are painful. As one pastor wrote on his survey, "This survey covers the greatest agonies of my life." If nothing else, this survey affirms once again the reality of temptation and the need to renew commitments to personal purity.

— Terry Muck
Senior Vice-President
Christianity Today, Inc.

PART I
THE PERSONAL
PERIL

Driving through Wisconsin on vacation, a LEADERSHIP *staff member passed a huge sign in the middle of the bucolic countryside. "Naughty Things for Nice People," it proclaimed, and as if to prove it, a gigantic cuddly bear peered out from beside the words "Adult Novelties."*

"What's that mean, Dad?" came the question from the 10-year-old boy in the back of the station wagon. "Yeah," piped up the siblings, "what's that all about, Dad?"

Such questions abound these days, as media penetrate our homes and station wagons with not just sleazy sex but carefully packaged titillations. One report has it that a recent convention of youth pastors prompted the most rentals of adult movies in the hotel's history. More than 80 percent of all customers signing up for cable TV opt for the erotic films. The availability — the near-ubiquity — of so much sexual enticement, the constant barrage of innuendoes, and the nonstop polemic for indulgence inevitably attracts.

Many rationales tempt the mind of the Christian leader: "I have to know what's going on. Voyeurism is better than adultery. I need moderation — total deprivation isn't necessary."

Admittedly, there are no easy answers. We cannot shut off either our brains or our glands. But consider the following chapters by individuals in full-time ministry. The chapters are blunt. But we felt it important to be just this blunt and realistic. Sexual temptations in many forms have always lured Christians, but today's opportunities and climate make this article especially relevant to all of us.

Chapter 1, "The War Within," is written by a Christian leader who prefers to remain anonymous so he can speak more personally and with more candor. This chapter was originally published as an article in LEADERSHIP in 1982.

Chapter 2, "Perils of the Professionally Holy," offers some thoughts about why those in ministry are particularly susceptible to sins of the body. It is written by Bill D. Hallsted, who ministers at the Truman (Minnesota) Church of Christ.

Chapter 3, "The War Within Continues," is written by the same anonymous writer who penned chapter 1, but was written five years later. It updates the continuing but hopeful battle against lust.

Chapter 4, "After the Affair," is the story of a pastor's wife whose husband confessed to a series of adulterous relationships. Heather Bryce is a pen name for this woman, who continues to live with her husband in the midwestern United States.

ONE

THE WAR WITHIN

Marriage does not remedy lust. If anything, it complicates the problem by introducing a new set of difficulties.

NAME WITHHELD

Lust is the ape that gibbers in our loins. Tame him as we will by day, he rages all the wilder in our dreams by night. Just when we think we're safe from him, he raises up his ugly head and smirks, and there's no river in the world flows cold and strong enough to strike him down. Almighty God, why dost thou deck men out with such a loathsome toy?

— Frederick Buechner
Godric

I am writing this anonymously because I am embarrassed. Embarrassed for my wife and children, yes, but embarrassed most for myself. I will tell of my personal battle with lust, and if I believed I were the only one who fought in that war, I would not waste emotional energy dredging up stained and painful memories. But I believe my experience is not uncommon, is perhaps even typical of pastors, writers, and conference speakers. No one talks about it. No one writes about it. But it's there, like an unacknowledged cancer that metastasizes best when no one goes for x-rays or feels for lumps.

I know I am not alone, because the few times I have opened up and shared my struggles with Christian friends, they have replied with Doppelgänger stories of exactly the same stages of awakening, obsession, possession. Years from now, when socio-historians sift through the documents describing our times, they will undoubtedly come up with elegant explanations of why men who grew up in church homes were over-sexed and vulnerable to attacks of lust and obsession, and why women who grew up in those same environments emerged uptight and somewhat disinterested in sex. But I leave that to the future analysts.

I remember vividly the night I first experienced lust. Real lust — not the high school and college variety. Of course as an adolescent I had drooled through *Playboy*, sneaked off to my uncle's room for a heart-thumping first look at hard-core pornography, and done my share of grappling and fumbling with my fiancee's clothes. I date my lust awakening, though, to the adult onslaught of mature, willful commitment to lust.

It hit on one of my first trips away from home. My job required me to travel at that time, and as I sat in a dingy motel room near the airport and flipped through the city guide of what to do in Rochester, New York, I kept coming back to one haunting photo of an exotic dancer, a former Miss Peach Bowl winner, the ad said. She looked fresh and inviting: the enchanting kind of Southern girl you see on TV commercials for fried chicken — only this one had no clothes on.

Somehow, I had survived the sixties sheltered from strippers and Woodstock-type nudity. And when I first saw the ad, I instinctively ruled her show out of bounds for me. But as I settled down to watch an inane TV show, her body kept looming before my mind with the simple question, "Why not?"

I began to think. Indeed, why not? To be an effective Christian, I had to experience all of life, right? Didn't Jesus himself hang around with prostitutes and sinners? I could go simply as an observer, in the world but not of the world. Rationalizations leaped up like flying buttresses to support my desires, and within ten minutes I was bundled in the back seat of a taxi headed toward the seamy side of Rochester.

I got the driver to let me off a few blocks away, just for safety's sake, and I kept glancing over my shoulder expecting to see someone I knew. Or perhaps God would step in, efface my desires, and change my mind about the wisdom of the act. I even asked him about that, meekly. No answer.

I walked into the bar between acts and was then faced with the new experience of ordering a drink. My forehead sweating, I scanned my memory of Westerns for an appropriate drink to order. Finally I decided on whiskey. I tried to make it sound casual, but the waitress flummoxed me by asking another question.

"How do you want it?"

How do I want it? What did she mean? What could I say? It seemed everyone in the bar was staring at me.

"A double," I stammered.

Sensing my naivete, she rolled her eyes slightly and asked, "Is on the rocks okay?"

Bolstered by my first fiery sips of whiskey, which I tried to stretch out so as not to have to order another, I sat with my eyes glued to the stage.

Miss Peach Bowl was everything the ad had promised. With a figure worthy of a Wonder Woman costume, she danced superbly and was something of an acrobat. She started fully clothed and teased us with slow removals of each sequined article of clothing. Toward the end, when she wore only a G-string, whooping men near the stage bade her lean over and stuffed folded bills under the tiny swatch of cloth. She grinned invitingly. I stared in disbelief. In one final strobe-lit routine she cartwheeled nude across the stage.

The flush of excitement created by my first whiskey, drunk too fast in spite of myself, the eye-popping spectacle of this gorgeous woman baring all and jiggling it in front of me, and the boisterous spirit of the all-male audience combined to overpower me. I walked out of the bar two hours later feeling strangely warmed, intensely excited, and surprised that nothing had actually happened to me. I suppose it's the same feeling that washes in after a big event like marriage, or graduation, or first intercourse for that matter. Afterward you realize that although in one sense everything has changed, in another sense nothing has changed. You are the same person.

Lust shares with sins like envy and pride the distinction of being invisible, slippery, hard to pin down. Was what happened that night a sin? I denied it to myself on the way home. To really rate as lust, I told myself, you must look on a woman so as to desire sexual intercourse with her. Isn't that what Jesus said? Whatever happened that night, I certainly couldn't recall desiring intercourse with Miss Peach Bowl. It was more private and distant than that. What happened, happened quickly, was gone, and left no scars. Or so I thought at the time.

Ten years have passed since that awakening in wintry Rochester, ten years spent never far from the presence of lust. The guilt caught up with me, and back in my motel room that very evening, I was already praying slobbery prayers for forgiveness. For a while that guilt kept me out of live shows and limited my voyeurism to magazines and movies, but only for a while. For ten years I have fought unremitting guerrilla warfare.

Being the reflective sort, I have often pondered the phenomenon of lust. It is unlike anything else in my experience. Most thrills — scary roller coasters, trips in airplanes, visits to waterfalls — lost a certain edge of excitement once I had experienced them and figured them out. I enjoy them and will duplicate the experiences if given the chance, but after a few tries, they no longer hold such a powerful gravitational attraction.

Sex is utterly different. There is only so much to "figure out." Every person who endures high school biology, let alone a sniggering sex education class, knows the basic shapes, colors, and sizes of the sexual organs. Anyone who has been to an art museum knows about women's breasts. Anyone who has hauled down a gynecology book in a public library knows about genitalia. Somehow, no amount of knowledge reduces the appeal — the forces may, in fact, work concordantly. What strange power is it that allows a male gynecologist to clinically examine female sexual organs all day long — there is nothing left for him to "learn" — and yet return home and find himself quickly aroused by his wife's peekaboo blouse?

"An ape that gibbers in my loins," wrote novelist Frederick Buechner about lust, and no experience comes with such a feral force. And yet, maybe by labeling it an "animal drive" we have missed the main point of lust. No animal I have heard of spends its life fixating on sex. Females in most species invite attention only a few times a year or less; the rest of the time males obediently plod through the mundane routine of phylogeny, apparently never giving sex another thought.

Humans are different. We have the freedom to center our lives inordinately in this one drive, without the harmony enforced by nature. Our females are biologically receptive the vast majority of the time, and no instinct inhibits us from focusing all our thoughts, behavior, and energy on sex.

I have tried to analyze lust, to fractionate it down into its particulars. I take a *Playboy* centerfold and study it with a magnifying glass. It consists only of dots — dots of four primary colors laid down by a printing press in a certain order. There is no magic on that page, only stipples of ink, which under magnification, show flaws and blurs. But there is magic on that page. I can stare at it, burn the image in my mind, fondle it mentally for hours, even days. Blood steams up when I gaze on it.

Early Marxists, heady with revolution, added sex to their list of human foibles needing alteration. Lenin pronounced his famous Glass of Water Theory, legislating that the sexual act was of no more consequence than the quenching of thirst by a glass of water. Surely bourgeois morality would topple along with bourgeois banks and industries and religions. But in a few years, Lenin had to abjure the Glass of Water Theory. By all reductionist logic, sex was like a glass of water, but sex proved immune to reductionist logic. It resisted being made of no consequence. Lenin, a historian, should have known better. Kings had renounced their thrones, saints their God, and spouses their lifetime partners because of this strange demon of lust. Dialectical materialism hardly stood a chance.

Books often question God's wisdom or goodness in allowing so much pain and sorrow in the world, and yet I have read none that question his goodness and wisdom in allowing so much sex and lust in the world. But I think the two may be parallel questions. Whether through creation or marred creation or whatever (we can't get into that here), we ended up with sex drives that virtually impel us to break rules God laid down. Males reach their sexual peak at age 18, scientists tell us. In our culture, you can't even legally marry before then, so when a male marries, if he has remained chaste, he has already forfeited his time of greatest sexual prowess. Mark Twain railed against God for parceling out to each human a source of universal joy and pleasure, at its peak in teenage years, then forbidding it until marriage and restricting it to one partner. He has a point.

Couldn't our hormones or chromosomes have been arranged so that mates would more easily find sexual satisfaction with just one partner? Why weren't we made more like the animals, who, except for specified periods, go through their daily routine (nude to a beast) with hardly a thought of sex. I could handle lust better if I knew it would only strike me in October or May. It's the not knowing, the ceaseless vulnerability, that drives me crazy.

Lust, I read somewhere, is the craving for salt by a man who is dying of thirst. There's a touch of perversion there, isn't there? Why were we not made with merely a craving for water, thus removing salt's attraction from every newsstand, television show, and movie?

I know what you are thinking. You are protesting that God never makes me lust, that I choose it, that he probably allows it as an opportunity for me to exercise my virtue. Yes, yes, I understand all that. But some of you know firsthand, as I do, that those pious platitudes, albeit perfectly correct, have almost no relevance to what happens biologically inside me when I visit a local beach or pick up any of a hundred magazines.

Some of you know what it is like to walk with your eyes at breast level, to flip eagerly through every new issue of *Time* searching for a rare sexy picture, to yearn for chains on the outside of your motel room to keep you in — unless it comes with that most perverse of all modern inventions, the in-room porno movie. And you also know what it is like to wallow in the guilt of that obsession, and to cry and pray with whatever faith you can muster, to plead with God to release you, to mutate you, to castrate you like Origen — whatever it takes to deliver you. And even as you pray, luscious, bewitching images crowd into your mind.

You also know what it is like to preach on Sunday, in a strange city, to preach even on a topic like grace or obedience or the will of God, or the decline of our civilization, with the awful and wonderful memories of last night's lust still more real to you at that moment than the sea of expectant faces spread out before you. You know the self-hatred that comes with that intolerable dissonance. And you muddle through the sermon swearing never to let it get to you like that again, until after the service a shapely woman comes beaming and squeezes your hand and whispers praise to you, and all resolve melts, and as she explains how blessed she was by your message, you are mentally undressing her.

The night in Rochester was my first experience with adult lust, but by no means my last. Strip joints are too handy these days. The drug store down the street sells *Hustler, High Society, Jugs,* anything you want. I have been to maybe fifteen truly pornographic movies, including the few classics like *Deep Throat* and *Behind the Green Door.* They scare me, perhaps because it seems so deliberate and volitional to stand in line (always glancing around furtively), to pay out money, and to sit in the dark for an hour or two. The crowd is unlike any other crowd I mix with — they remind me I don't belong. And the movies, technically, aesthetically, and even erotically, are vapid and boring. But still, when a local paper advertises one more *Emmanuelle* sequel, I drool.

I learned quickly that lust, like physical sex, points in only one direction. You cannot go back to a lower level and stay satisfied. Always you want more. A magazine excites, a movie thrills, a live show really makes the blood run. I never got as far as body tattooing, personal photograph sessions, and massages, let alone outright prostitution, but I experienced enough of the unquenchable nature of sex to frighten me for good. Lust does not satisfy; it stirs up. I no longer wonder how deviants can get into child molesting, masochism, and other abnormalities. Although such acts are incomprehensible to me, I remember well that where I ended up was also incomprehensible to me when I started.

A cousin of mine subscribes to at least fifteen of the raunchiest magazines I have ever seen. Books I have peeked at for just a few seconds in airport newsstands litter his house. He has told me that, even surrounded by vivid depictions of every sex act, every size and shape of woman he can imagine, he still wants more. He still devours the new issues. He and his wife are experimenting with orgies now, and numerous other variations I won't mention. It is not enough. The thrill will fade before long, and he will want more.

Psychologists use the term *obsession* to label what I have been describing, and they may say that I have more innate obsession than the average male. They would trace its genesis back to my repressive upbringing, and they are undoubtedly right. That is why I am writing to others of you in the Christian world. If you have not fought such obsession yourself, every Sunday when you step to the pulpit you speak to many who have, although you could hardly read it in their blank, freshly scrubbed faces. Lust is indeed an invisible sin.

At times the obsession has felt to me more like possession. I remember one time especially that scared me. I was in Washington, D.C., one of the places in the United States where any kind of lust is easily attainable. At three o'clock in the afternoon, after touring the cherry blossoms, I sauntered into a dark bar that advertised nude dancing. I fended off the girls who came to my table and asked for drinks, and instead directed my attention to the dancers. There were only two, and maybe five customers at most. One black girl with an unspectacular figure weaved over to the part of the stage nearest my table.

This was somewhat different than the other strip shows I had seen. There was no teasing or "visual foreplay." She was already naked, unashamedly so, and she wiggled maybe a foot from my head. She stared right into my eyes. This was so close, so intimate, that it seemed for a terrifying moment to be nearer a relationship than a performance. What I felt could only be called possession.

I found myself — it seemed as though I had not made the decision, that someone else's hand inside mine was doing it — fumbling in my pocket, pulling out bills and stuffing them in a garter belt high up on her thigh. In appreciation she maneuvered herself to grant an even better view. She had no secrets.

I staggered out of that bar. I felt I had crossed a line and could never return to innocence. That weekend I had important business engagements, but throughout them indelible images of that anonymous girl filled my mind. I yearned to flee and go home to my wife, to demonstrate to her my fear so that she could shelter me and mother me and keep me from following where all this was leading.

Just a few years before, I had sat with a distant, reproachful view and watched men lose control and act like country-fair churls as they stuffed bills down the G-string of Miss Peach Bowl. I would never stoop to that — I was smugly confident in Rochester. After all, I was intelligent, happily married, sophisticated — a committed Christian known by friends for my self-control. It would never happen. But it did.

When I went home, I did not tell my wife. How could I? The

story was too long, and she, who had hardly ever known lust and had never been unfaithful to me, would not comprehend it. It would likely rupture my marriage, and then I would be cast loose on a sea I could not navigate.

I made a vow then — one more in a series. I vowed I would only look at *Playboy* and other "respectable" erotic magazines. No more raunchiness. I had certain rationalizations about lust, and pained realism about my inability to stay pure. I simply needed some safe boundaries, I decided. Here are some of my rationalizations that supported my conclusion to contain, not destroy, my lust:

● Nudity is art. Go to any museum in the world, and you will see nudity openly displayed. The human form is beautiful, and it would be puritanical to cut off appreciation for it. *Playboy* is photographed well, with an aesthetic, not prurient tone.

● *Playboy* and its kin have great articles. There's the Jimmy Carter interview, for example, and *Penthouse's* conversation with Jerry Falwell. I must keep up with such material.

● Some stimulation will help my sex life. I have a problem approaching my wife and communicating my desire for sex to her. I need a sort of boost, a stimulant to push me to declare my intentions.

● Other people do far worse. I know many Christian leaders who still do all the things I toyed with, and worse. For that matter, look at Bible characters — as randy a bunch as you'll ever meet. There's probably no such thing as a pure person anyway; everybody has some outlet.

● What is lust anyhow, I kept asking myself. Is fantasizing wrong in itself? If so, then erotic dreams would count as sin, and how could I be responsible for my dreams? I reminded myself of the definition of lust I had started with long before: desiring intercourse with a specific sexual partner. I experienced a general sexual heightening, a raising of the voltage, not a specific desire for the act of intercourse.

Some, perhaps all, of these rationalizations contain some truth. (Do they sound familiar?) I used them as an overlay of reason and common sense to help calm the cognitive dissonance that tormented me. Yet I knew inside that the lust I experienced was not subject to reason and common sense. To my dismay, on several occasions I had already felt it burst out of containment and take on a sinister power. At other times, I could analyze lust and put it in perspective, but at the moment when it was occurring I knew I would not stop and analyze. I would let it take its course. Secretly, I began to wonder what that course would be.

Don't let me give the wrong impression. My entire life did not revolve around lust. I would go days without fixating on sex, and sometimes a month or two without seeking out a pornographic magazine or movie. And many, many times I would cry out to God, imploring him to take away the desire. Why were my prayers not answered? Why did God continue to curse me with freedom, even when that freedom led me away from him?

I read numerous articles and books on temptation but found little help. If you boiled down all the verbiage and the ten-point lists of practical advice for coping with temptation, basically all they said was "Just stop doing it." That was easy to say. I knew some of those authors, and knew that they too struggled and failed, as I did. In fact, I too had preached many a sermon on handling temptation, but look at me. Practical "how-to" articles proved hopelessly inadequate, as if they said "Stop being hungry" to a starving man. Intellectually I might agree with their theology and their advice, but my glands would still secrete. What insight can change glands?

"Jesus was tempted in all points as you are," some of the articles and books would say, as if that would cheer me up. It did not help. In the first place, none of the authors could possibly describe how Jesus experienced sexual temptation, because he never talked about it, and no one else has ever been perfect. Such well-meaning comments reminded me of telling a ghetto dweller in East Bronx, "Oh, I used to be poor, too. I know how you feel." Try telling that to a poor person, and prepare to duck.

I felt a similar reaction when I read accounts of people who had overcome lust. Usually, they wrote or talked in a condescending, unctuous tone. Or, like Jesus, they seemed too far removed from my own spiritual quagmire to comfort me. Augustine described his condition twelve years after conversion from his lusty state. In that advanced spiritual place he prayed to overcome these besetting sins: the temptation to enjoy his food instead of taking it as a necessary medicine "until the day when Thou wilt destroy both the belly and the meat"; the attraction of sweet scents; the pleasure of the ear provided by church music lest he be "more moved by the singing than by the thing that is sung"; the lure of the eye to "diverse forms of beauty, of brilliant and pleasing colors"; and last, the temptation of "knowing for knowing's sake." Sorry, Augustine, I respect you, but prayers like that led to the climate of repression and body-hatred that I have been vainly trying to escape all my life.

I got a perverse pleasure out of knowing that this same Augustine a few years earlier had prayed, "Give me chastity, but not yet." He delayed purity for a while also, to sample more delights than I would likely get around to. Why is it that I scoffed at accounts of saints who overcame temptation but loved hearing about those who gave in? There must be a name for that sin, too.

Most of this time I hated sex. I could not imagine it existing in any sort of balance in my life. Of course I knew its pleasure — that *was* the gravitational attraction — but those short bursts of pleasure were horribly counterbalanced by days of guilt and anguish. I could not reconcile my technicolor fantasy life with my more mundane experience of sex in marriage. I began to view sex as another of God's mistakes, like tornadoes and earthquakes. In the final analysis, it only caused misery. Without it, I could conceive of becoming pure and godly and all those other things the Bible exhorted me toward. With sex, any spiritual development seemed hopelessly unattainable. Maybe Origen had the right idea after all.

It is true there is difficulty in entering into godliness. But this difficulty does not arise from the religion which begins in us, but only from the irreligion which is still there. If our senses were not opposed to penitence, and if our corruption were not opposed to the purity of God, there would be nothing in this painful to us. We suffer only in proportion as the vice which is natural to us resists supernatural grace. Our heart feels torn asunder between these opposed efforts. But it would be very unfair to impute this violence to God, who is drawing us on, instead of to the world, which is holding us back. It is as a child, which a mother tears from the arms of robbers, in the pain it suffers, should love the loving and legitimate violence of her who procures its liberty, and detest only the impetuous and tyrannical violence of those who detain it unjustly. The most cruel war which God can make with men in this life is to leave them without that war which He came to bring. "I came to send war," He says, "and to teach them of this war. I came to bring fire and the sword." Before Him the world lived in this false peace.

— Blaise Pascal
Pensees

This chapter is divided into two parts. The first part, which you have just read, recounts the downward spiral of temptation, yielding, self-hatred, and despair. If I had read this article several years ago, I would have gleefully affirmed everything. Then, when I got to the second part, which describes a process of healing, I would have turned cynical and sour, rejecting what follows. Such is the nature of self-deception.

I have described my slide in some detail not to feed any prurient interests in the reader and certainly not to nourish your own despair if you too are floundering — God forbid. I tell my struggles because they are real, but also to demonstrate that hope exists, that God is alive, and his grace can interrupt the terrible cycle of lust and despair. My primary message is one of hope, although until healing did occur, I had no faith that it ever would.

Scores, maybe hundreds of times I had prayed for deliverance, with no response. The theologians would find some fault in my prayers, or in the faith with which I prayed them. But can any person assume the awful right to judge the prayers of another who writhes in mental torment and an agony of helpless unspirituality? I would certainly never assume the right, not after a decade-long war against lust.

I have not mentioned the effect of lust on my marriage. It did not destroy my marriage, did not push me out to find more sexual excitation in an adulterous affair, or with prostitutes, did not even impel me to place unrealistic demands on my wife's sexual performance. The effect was far more subtle. Mainly, I think, it cumulatively caused me to devalue my wife as a sexual being. The great lie promulgated by *Playboy*, television commercials, and racy movies is that the physical ideal of beauty is attainable and oh, so close. I stare at a *Playboy* centerfold. Miss October has such a warm, inviting smile. She is with me alone, in my living room. She removes her clothes, just for me, and lets me see all of her. She tells me about her favorite books and what she likes in a man. Cheryl Tiegs, in the famous *Sports Illustrated* swimsuit issue, sweetly walks toward the camera, letting the coral blush of her breasts shine out boldly from underneath a fishnet bikini. She lets me see them — she has no inhibitions, no pudency.

The truth is, of course, that if I sat next to either Cheryl Tiegs or Miss October on an airplane, she would not give me the time of day, let alone take off her clothes for me. If I tried to strike up a conversation, she would brush me off. And yet, because I have stared at Cheryl's breasts and gone over every inch of Miss October as well as the throng of beauties that Madison Avenue and Hollywood recruit to tantalize the masses, I start to view my own wife in that light. I expect her to have Farrah's smile, Cheryl's voluptuousness, Angie's legs, Miss October's flaming red hair and sparkling eyes. Envy and greed join hands with lust. I begin to focus on my wife's minor flaws. I lose sight of the fact that she is a charming, warm, attractive woman and that I am fortunate to have found her.

Beyond that, lust affected my marriage in an even more subtle and pernicious way. Over time, I began to view sex schizophrenically. Sex in marriage was one thing. We performed okay, though not as often as I liked, and accompanied by typical misunderstandings. But passion, ah, that was something different. Passion I never felt in my marriage.

If anything, sex within marriage served as an overflow valve, an outlet for the passion that mounted inside me, fed by sources kept hidden from my wife. We never talked about this, yet I am sure she sensed it. I think she began to view herself as a sex object — not in the feminist sense of being the object of a husband's selfish greed, but in the deprived sense of being only the object of my physical necessity and not of romance and passion.

Yet the sexual schizophrenia pales in comparison to the schizophrenia of my spiritual life. Can you imagine the inner rupture when I would lead a spiritual retreat for a weekend, winning sighs of admiration and tears of commitment from my devoted listeners, only to return to my room and pore over the latest copy of *Oui*? I could never reconcile it, but somehow I could not avoid it. If you pinned me down on what degree my succumbing to temptation was a conscious choice, I would probably search for an enigmatic response such as the one a Faulkner character gave when asked about original sin. "Well, it's like this," he said. "I ain't got to, but I can't help it."

Paradoxically, I seemed most vulnerable to temptation when speaking or otherwise performing some spiritual service. Those who see Satan as personally manipulating all such temptation to sin would not be surprised by that observation.

Lust became the one corner of my life that God could not enter. I welcomed him into the area of personal finance, which he revolutionized as I awakened to world needs. He cleaned up many of my personal relationships. He gave stirrings of life to the devotional area and my sense of personal communion with him. But lust was sealed off, a forbidden room. How can I reconcile that statement with my earlier protestations that I often cried out for deliverance? I do not know. I felt both sensations: an overwhelming desire to be cleansed and an overwhelming desire to cling to the exotic pleasure of lust. A magnet is attracted equally to two opposite forces. No matter how small you cut a magnet or rearrange it, the two ends will still be attracted to opposite forces. One force never cancels out the other one. This must be what Paul meant in some of those strange statements in Romans 7 (a passage that gave me some comfort). But where was Romans 8 in my life?

Even when I had lust under control, when I successfully limited it to brief, orderly perusals through *Playboy* at the local newsstand, I still felt this sense of retaining a secret corner God could not enter. Often I would get bogged down in sermon preparation. For motivation to keep going, I would promise myself a trip to the newsstand if I could finish the sermon in an hour and a half. Can you sense the schizophrenia?

Just as I can remember graphically the precise incident in Rochester when adult lust moved in, I can remember the first flutterings of a commitment to healing. They also came on a trip out of town, when I was speaking at a spiritual-life conference. The conference was scheduled for a resort hotel in the White Mountains of New Hampshire, near my favorite part of the country. Nothing affects me like the long drive up the rocky coastline of Maine. It is an invigorating, almost religious experience. Some people find deserts affect them like that, some wheat fields, and some mountains. For me, the magnificence of creation unwinds with each curve on the road up Maine's coast. I made plans to fly into Boston, rent a car, and spend three days cruising the coast just to refresh myself before the conference.

My mistake was spending the first night in Boston. I was then practicing a fairly rigid regiment of "controlled lust." I hadn't given in to any scary splurges like my Washington, D.C. encounter in some time. But sure enough, that night I found myself stalking the streets of the seedy areas looking for temptation. I did not have to look far. Like many cities, Boston offers strip shows, porno movies — a veritable menu of lust. I usually avoided porno movies because they had proved so unsatisfying. But, Boston also features live nude girls on a revolving platform that you can watch for twenty-five cents. I went in one of those booths.

The mechanics are simple. Twenty curtained booths encircle a revolving platform. Each booth has a glass window covered by a piece of plywood. When you insert a quarter, a mechanical arm somewhat like a toll gate lowers the piece of plywood and lets you see the nude girls revolving on the platform. Then, about three minutes later the toll gate goes up, and you have to drop in another quarter to continue. This is lust at its most unadorned.

The girls employed by such places are not beautiful. Imagine for yourself what kind of women would willingly settle for such employment. You lie under bright lights, revolving like a piece of roast beef at a buffet table, masturbating occasionally to keep the quarters clinking. Around you, leering, furtive stares of men appear for three minutes, then disappear, then appear again, their glasses reflecting your pale shape, none of them looking at your face.

Maybe such booths do serve a redeeming purpose for society — by exposing lust in its basest demythologized form. There is no art or beauty, no acrobatic dancing. The woman is obviously a sex object and nothing else. The men are isolated, caged voyeurs. There is no relationship, no teasing.

The girls are bored stiff: over the whir of the timing mechanism you can hear them trading talk about grocery prices or car repairs. They masturbate as a routine for the customers, like an ape at the zoo who learns to make faces because the onlookers then laugh and point. This is what the richest, freest society in history spends its wealth and freedom on?

And yet, there I was, a respected member of that society, three days away from leading a spiritual-life retreat, dropping in quarters like a frantic long-distance caller at a pay phone.

For fifty cents you could go to a private booth, and one of the girls would entertain you personally. A glass wall still separated you from the girl, but you could, if you wished, pick up the receiver and talk to the girl. Maybe you could talk her into doing something special for you. I went into the booth, but something restrained me from picking up the telephone. I could not make that human an act — it would expose me for what I was. I merely stood, silent, and stared.

Guilt and shame washed over me in waves that night, as usual. Again I had a stark picture of how low I was groveling. Did this animal lust have any relation to the romance that had inspired the *Symphonie Fantastique*, Elizabeth Barrett Browning's *Sonnets*, and the Song of Solomon? Certainly each of those works contained traces of glandular desire, but what I had experienced was devoid of all beauty. It was too naked, and shameful.

I had felt all that remorse before. What shocked me more was my trip up the coast the next two days. I followed my usual practice of staying in homey inns with big fireplaces, and of eating by the waterfront and watching the sailboats bob in the shimmering sea, of taking long solitary walks on the rocky promontories where huge waves crashed with thunder, of closing my eyes and letting salt spray splash across my face, of stopping at roadside stands for fresh lobster and crab. There was a difference this time: I felt no pleasure. None. My emotional reaction was the same as if I had been at home, yawning, reading the newspaper. All romance had drained out, desiccated.

The realization disturbed me profoundly. By all counts, those wonderful, sensuous experiences rated far higher than the cheap thrill of watching a fat, pock-marked body rotate on plywood. And yet, to my utter disbelief my mind kept roaming back to that grimy booth in Boston. Was I crazy? Would I lose every worthwhile sensation in life? Was my soul leaking away? Was I becoming possessed?

I limped through the conference, and everyone warmly applauded each talk. They were all blessed. Alone in my room at night, I did not pore over pornography. I pored over what had been happening inside me for ten years. I did not like it.

Exactly three days later, I spent the night with a very dear friend, a pastor of one of the largest churches in the South. I had never shared intimate details of my lust life with anyone before, but the schizophrenia was building to such a point I felt I must. He listened quietly, with compassion and great sensitivity as I recounted a few incidents, skipping over those that showed me in the worst light, and described some of my fears to him.

He sat for a long time with sad eyes after I had finished speaking. We both watched our freshly refilled cups of coffee steam, then stop steaming, then grow cold. I waited for his words of advice or comfort or healing or something. I needed a priest at that moment, someone to say, "Your sins are forgiven."

But my friend was no priest. He did something I never expected. His lip quivered at first, the skin on his face began twitching, and finally he started sobbing — great, huge, wretched sobs such as I had seen only at funerals.

In a few moments, when he had recovered some semblance of self-control, I learned the truth. My friend was not sobbing for me; he was sobbing for himself. He began to tell me of his own expedition into lust. He had been where I was — five years before. Since that time, he had taken lust to its logical consequences. I will not dwell on sordid details, but my friend had tried it all: bondage, prostitution, bisexualism, orgies. He reached inside his vest pocket and pulled out a pad of paper showing the prescriptions he took to fight the venereal disease and anal infections he had picked up along the way. He carries the pad with him on trips, he explained, to buy the drugs in cities where he is anonymous.

I saw my friend dozens of times after that and learned every horrific detail of his hellish life. I worried about cognitive dissonance; he brooded on suicide. I read about deviance; he performed it. I winced at subtle fissures in my marriage; he was in divorce litigation.

I could not sit in judgment of this man, because he had simply ended up where my own obsession would likely take me. Jesus brought together lust and adultery, hatred and murder, in the Sermon on the Mount, not to devalue adultery and murder but rather to point to the awesome truth about hatred and lust. There is a connection.

If I had learned about my friend's journey to debauchery in a book like this one, I doubtless would have clucked my tongue, questioned the editor's judgment in printing it, and rejected the author as an insincere poseur in the faith. But I knew this man, I thought, as well as I knew anyone. His insights, compassion, and love were all more mature than mine. My sermons were like freshman practice runs compared to his. He was a godly man if I had ever met one, but underneath all that . . . my inner fear jumped uncontrollably. I sensed the power of evil.

For some weeks I lived under a cloud that combined the feelings of doom and terror. Had I crossed some invisible line so that my soul was stained forever? Would I too, like my trusted friend, march inexorably toward the systematic destruction of my body and soul? He had cried for forgiveness, and deliverance, and every other prayer he had learned in church, and yet now he had fallen into an abyss. Already lawyers were dividing up his house and possessions and children. Was there no escape for him — for me?

My wife could sense the inner tension, but in fifteen years of marriage she had learned not to force a premature explanation. I had not learned to share tension while it was occurring, only afterward, when it fit into a logical sequence, with some sort of resolution. This time, I wondered whether this particular problem would ever have such a resolution.

A month after my conversation with my friend, I began reading a brief and simple book of memoirs, *What I Believe*, by François Mauriac. In it, he sums up why he clung to the Roman Catholic church and Christian faith in a country (France) and an age when few of his contemporaries seriously considered orthodoxy. I had read only one novel by the Nobel prize-winning author, *Viper's Tangle*, but that novel clearly showed that Mauriac fully understood the lust I had experienced, and more. A great artist, he had captured the depths of human depravity. I would not get pious answers from him.

Mauriac's book includes one chapter on purity. He describes the power of sexuality — "the sexual act has no resemblance to any other act: its demands are frenzied and participate in infinity. It is a tidal wave" — and his struggles with it throughout a strict Catholic upbringing. He also discounts common evangelical perspectives on lust and sex. The experience of lust and immorality, he admits, is fully pleasurable and desirable; it is no good trying to pretend that sin contains distasteful seeds that inevitably grow into repulsion. Sin has its own compelling rewards. Even marriage, Christian marriage, he claims, does not remedy lust. If anything, marriage complicates the problem by introducing a new set of difficulties. Lust continues to seek the attraction of unknown creatures and the taste for adventure and chance meetings.

After brazenly denying the most common reasons I have heard against succumbing to a life filled with lust, Mauriac concludes that there is only one reason to seek purity. It is the reason Christ proposed in the Beatitudes: "Blessed are the pure in heart, for they shall see God." Purity, says Mauriac, is the condition for a higher love — for a possession superior to all possessions: God himself.

Mauriac goes on to describe how most of our arguments for purity are negative arguments: Be pure, or you will feel guilty, or your marriage will fail, or you will be punished. But the Beatitudes clearly indicate a positive argument that fits neatly with the Bible's pattern in describing sins. Sins are not a list of petty irritations drawn up for the sake of a jealous God. They are, rather, a description of the impediments to spiritual growth. We are the ones who suffer if we sin, by forfeiting the development of character and Christlikeness that would have resulted if we had not sinned.

The thought hit me like a bell rung in a dark, silent hall. So far, none of the scary, negative arguments against lust had succeeded in keeping me from it. Fear and guilt simply did not give me resolve; they added self-hatred to my problems. But here was a description of what I was missing by continuing to harbor lust: I was limiting my own intimacy with God. The love he offers is so transcendent and possessing that it requires our faculties to be purified and cleansed before we can possibly contain it. Could he, in fact, substitute another thirst and another hunger for the one I had never filled? Would Living Water somehow quench lust? That was the gamble of faith.

Perhaps Mauriac's point seems obvious and predictable to people who respond to anguished problems with spiritual-sounding cliches. But I knew Mauriac and his life well enough to know that his observation was the culmination of a lifetime of struggle. He had come to that conclusion as the only possible justification for abstention. Perhaps, just perhaps, the discipline and commitment involved in somehow allowing God to purge out the impurities formed the *sine qua non*, the essential first step toward a relationship with God I had never known.

The combination of grave fear struck in me by my pastor friend's grievous story and the glimmer of hope that a quest for purity could somehow transform the hunger I had lived with unabated for a decade prepared me to try once again to approach God in confession and in faith. I knew pain would come. Could God this time give me assurance that, in Pascal's words, pain was the "loving and legitimate violence" necessary to procure my liberty?

I cannot tell you why a prayer that has been prayed for ten years is answered on the 1,000th request when God has met the first 999 with silence. I cannot tell you why I had to endure ten years of near-possession before being ready for deliverance. And, most sadly of all, I cannot tell you why my pastor friend has, since our conversation, gone into an unbelievable skid toward destruction. His marriage is now destroyed. He may go insane or commit suicide before this book is published. Why? I do not know.

But what I can tell you, especially those of you who have hung on every turn of my own pilgrimage because it so closely corresponds to yours, is that God did come through for me. The phrase may sound heretical, but to me, after so many years of failure, it felt as if he had suddenly decided to be there after a long absence. I prayed, hiding nothing (hide from God?), and he heard me.

There was one painful but necessary step of repentance. Repentance, says C. S. Lewis, "is not something God demands of you before He will take you back and which He could let you off if He chose; it is simply a description of what going back is like." Going back for me had to include a very long talk with my wife, who had suffered in silence and often in nescience for a decade. It was she I had wronged and sinned against, as well as God. Perhaps my impurity had kept our own love from growing in the same way it had blocked the love I could experience with God. We lay side by side on our bed one steamy summer evening. I talked about nothing, in a nervous, halting voice, for an hour or so, trying to break the barrier that held me back, and finally about midnight I began.

I told her nearly everything, knowing I was laying on her a burden she might not be able to carry. I have wondered why God let me struggle for a decade before deliverance: maybe I will one day find out my wife required just that much time to mature and prepare for the one talk we had that night. Far smaller things had fractured our marriage for months. Somehow, she incarnated the grace of God for me.

I hurt her — only she could tell how much I hurt her. It was not adultery — there was no other woman for her to beam her resentment toward, but perhaps that made it even harder for her. For ten years she had watched an invisible fog steal inside me, make me act strangely, pull me away from her. Now she heard what she had often suspected, and to her it must have sounded like rejection: You were not enough for me sexually, I had to go elsewhere.

But still, in spite of that pain and the vortex of emotions that must have swirled around inside her, she gave to me forgiveness and love. She took on my enemy as her enemy too. She took on my thirst for purity as her thirst too. She loved me, and as I type this even now, tears streak my face because that love, that awesome love is so incomprehensible to me, and so undeserved. But it was there.

How can I give you up, O Ephraim?
How can I hand you over, O Israel? . . .
For I am God and not man,
The Holy One in your midst.

— Hosea 11:8-9

Saint Augustine, who wrote so eloquently of his own war within, describes our condition here on earth as a simultaneous citizenship in two cities, the city of man and the City of God. The lure of the city of man often drowns out the call of the City of God. Man's city is visible, substantial, real; as such, it is far more alluring. God's city is ephemeral, invisible, cloaked in doubt, far away.

Cheryl Tiegs coming toward me out of the page, her teeth flashing, her eyes sparkling, her body glistening, is that city of man. She, and what she represents, fits well with my body and the hormones that surge inside it and the complexes that grew in my repressed childhood and whatever else contributed to my obsession with lust. The pure in heart shall see God. Set against luscious Cheryl, sometimes that promise does not seem like much. But that is the lie of the Deceiver, and the dyslexia of reality we are asked to overcome. The City of God is the real, the substantial, the whole. What I become as I strengthen my citizenship in that kingdom is far more worthy than anything I could become if all my fantasies were somehow fulfilled.

A year has passed since the late-night talk with my wife. During that time, a miracle has occurred. The war within me has fallen away. Only a few snipers remain. Once I failed, just a month later, when I was walking the streets of San Francisco. I felt myself pulled — it felt exactly like that — into another of the twenty-five cent peep shows to watch an undulating girl on a revolving table for three minutes. Not ten seconds had passed when I felt a sense of horror. My head was pounding. Evil was taking over. I had to get out of there, immediately.

I ran, literally ran, as fast as I could out of the North Beach district. I felt safe only when I got out of there. It struck me then how much had changed: previously I had felt safe when I had given in to lust, because the war inside died down for a moment, but now I felt safe away from the temptation. I prayed for strength and walked away.

Other than that encounter, I have been free of the compulsion. Of course, I notice girls in short dresses and halter tops — why else would they wear them? — but the terror is gone. The gravitational force has disappeared when I pass in front of newsstands. For twelve months I have walked by them and not picked up a magazine. I have not entered a porno theater.

I feel a sense of loss, yes. I enjoyed the beautiful women, both the art and the lust of it. It was pleasurable; I cannot deny that. But now I have gained a kind of inner gyroscope that is balanced correctly and alerts me when I am straying off course. After ten years I finally have a reservoir of strength to draw on as well as a conscience. I have found it necessary to keep open and honest communication with God and my wife on every little temptation toward lust.

The war within still exists. Now it is a war against the notion that biology is destiny. Looking at humanity as a species, scientists conclude that the fittest must survive, that qualities such as beauty, intelligence, strength, and skill are worthy factors by which to judge the usefulness of people, that lust is an innate adaptation to assure the propagation of the species. Charity, compassion, love, and restraint fly in the face of that kind of materialist philosophy. Sometimes they defy even our own bodies. The City of God can seem like a mirage; my battle is to allow God to convince me of its reality.

Two totally new experiences have happened to me that, I must admit, offset by far my sense of loss from avoiding lust.

First, I have learned that Mauriac was right. God has kept

his part of the bargain. In a way I had never known before, I have come to see God. At times (not so often, maybe once every couple of months), I have had an experience with God that has stunned me with its depth and intimacy, an experience of an order I did not even know existed before. Some of these moments have come during prayer and Bible reading, some during deep conversations with other people, and one, the most memorable of all because of my occupation, while I was speaking at a Christian conference. At such moments I have felt possessed, but this time joyfully so (demonic possession is a poor parody of the filling of the Spirit). They have left me shaken and humbled, renewed and cleansed. I had not known that level of mystical experience, had not, in fact, even sought it except in the general way of seeking purity. God has revealed himself to me. The City of God is taking on bricks and mortar.

And another thing has happened, again something I did not even ask God for. The passion is coming back into my marriage. My wife is again becoming an object of romance. *Her* body, no one else's, is gradually gaining the gravitational pull that used to be scattered in the universe of sexes. The act of sex, as often a source of irritation and trauma for me as an experience of pleasure, is beginning to take on the form of mystery and transcendence and inexpressible delight that its original design must have called for.

These two events occurring in such short sequence have shown me why the mystics, even some biblical writers, tend to employ the experience of sexual intimacy as a metaphor of spiritual ecstasy. Sometimes, lingering remnants of grace in the city of man bear a striking resemblance to what awaits us in the City of God.

TWO

PERILS OF THE PROFESSIONALLY HOLY

We who ought to hate sin more than anyone because we so constantly see its devastating effect can become the most blasé toward it.

BILL D. HALLSTED

Her face was convulsed with emotion as tears ran down her cheeks, her hands twisting a forgotten handkerchief into a tight knot. She finally choked out the reason she wouldn't go near church: "I was baptized almost seven years ago. The preacher had called and convinced me that's what I needed to do. We went right to the church, just the two of us, and he baptized me. Then he came into my dressing room and made a pass at me!"

As she told me her story, I was shocked. An extreme event? Yes. Appalling? Yes. Atypical? Yes, but sadly not a unique or isolated occurrence. Even some of the churches I've been associated with have had to ask for a preacher's resignation because of sexual misconduct.

So why the sexual failings, especially among ministers? A lack of Christian devotion or sincerity is rarely to blame. I suspect something more insidious is behind the problem. I've noticed three subtle but powerful dangers that cause extra temptation for the "professionally religious":

● *Overfamiliarity with God.* It's hardly possible to be too close to God. But it *is* possible to become so accustomed to the reality of God that we no longer stand in awe of him.

As preachers, our times of worship are easily identified

with work. Our recreation, much of it, is wrapped up in church activities. Our career is the church; our homes are often the property of the church. Our amusement, our jokes, our funny anecdotes and ironic remembrances, our comic relief — all center on the church. We handle the things of God day in and day out.

Because of this, we may begin to lose the awe that keeps us in profound respect of the holy and righteous God who will judge his people.

● *Sin saturation.* Compounding this tendency is our constant traffic with a numbing array of people's sins. Rightly we speak of God's boundless forgiveness and willingness to restore. But week after week, a torrent of sins needing forgiveness flows past our awareness until we may begin to lose sense of the awfulness of sin. We who ought to hate sin more than anyone because we so constantly see its devastating effect can become the most blasé toward it.

We've seen so many gross sins that when we are then tempted, it may seem such a minor thing if we, too, should sin: *All that forgiveness will surely cover me, won't it?*

● *Job overload.* It seems close to blasphemy to say we need time away from the things of God. Maybe that's why so many are unwilling to say it, let alone secure it.

Everyone else needs a break from thinking about jobs and the demands of work. Since our "job" surrounds us with the things of God, our minds need a similar rest. It's only natural.

Yet so much do our minds need a hiatus from constant religious exposure that we can find ourselves vulnerable to amusement far removed from the things of God, and our society offers limitless opportunities for such escape. They're as close as the television knob, the magazine rack, or the bookstore. And they sully the hands of God's workers.

The answer? A devotional pattern that places us starkly in awe before a fearsome God. A God-angled view of sin and its consequences. A habit of escaping the pressures of Christian work for relaxation and renewal — activities that don't violate the holiness of God.

Easy? Not at all, but necessary.

THREE

THE WAR WITHIN CONTINUES

Ironically, I am most grateful for two things I normally try to avoid: guilt and fear . . . yet guilt and fear are such powerful forces that they may also deceive. In my case, they deceived me into seeing God as my enemy.

Virtue, unlike innocence, has successfully passed a point of temptation.

NAME WITHHELD

I was sitting in an aisle seat on a cross-country flight when the passenger across the aisle, one row ahead, pulled out a magazine from his briefcase. I recognized something familiar in the furtive way he looked around, nervously adjusted his posture, and opened the magazine. He held the pages open just far enough to see inside, but from my angle I had a clear view of various women spreading their legs for the camera.

It seemed incongruous, even bizarre, for a man dressed in a business suit to be studying some anonymous woman's private parts in the artificial setting of jammed-together airplane seats and plastic folding trays. But after the sense of the bizarre had passed, I felt another twinge, this one a mixture of pain and sadness. Five years ago, I was that man in the business suit, addicted to lust. I wrote about my struggle in the Fall 1982 edition of LEADERSHIP, in an article called "The War Within," which also is Chapter 1 in this book. After the sadness had passed, I felt an enormous sense of relief, for I realized that my initial sense of bizarreness was a sign of the healing God has accomplished so far.

Not long after the airplane trip, an editor from LEADERSHIP asked if I would do another article, recounting what I had learned about lust in the five intervening years. At first, I didn't like the idea. It seemed an unnecessary probing of old wounds. The article had been for me a means of catharsis, a deliverance. Why dredge up the past? Finally, however, I agreed to consider the request.

I reread the original article for the first time in five years. Its passionate tone startled me. I had forgotten how completely sex had dominated my life. I found myself feeling compassion for the author of the article, momentarily forgetting his identity! Again, I breathed a prayer of thanks for God's healing. In the same file folder as the article, I also found an envelope from LEADERSHIP containing several dozen letters from readers, and I proceeded to read each one.

Some readers felt a sense of shock and betrayal. They criticized the article for being prurient and disgusting. The author had been far too explicit, they said; he dwelt on lurid details as if he still enjoyed his memories of lust.

"The author cannot possibly be considered a Christian," concluded one reader (I hope this person never encounters Augustine's *Confessions*). Others claimed the article had caused them to distrust their pastor and all Christian leaders: "Who knows what might be going on in their minds?"

I pray and hope that my article did not lead anyone astray. I must admit that, at a distance of five years, the article seemed somewhat overwrought. Does the issue of lust merit such a long, involved treatment? But I also know that the article was true, every word of it. I lived it. War raged within me for a decade.

At the time, some people were scandalized that a Christian magazine would print such a blunt, realistic confession by a Christian leader. But in more recent days we have read far more explicit accounts of Christian leaders' immorality in *Time* and *Newsweek*.

Not all the letters were negative, however. More than half expressed deep gratitude. I have a whole stack of letters that begin like this: "I thought I was the only one with this problem. Thank you so much for having the courage to bring it out into the open." Some go on to describe agonizing personal battles with lust and immorality. At least one reader said the article permanently cured his lust problem by frightening him away from the temptations of bare flesh.

The most moving letters, however, came from people who have not been cured. "Please, tell me how to solve my problem!" they wrote. "You said that God 'came through' for you, but he has not come through for me. What can I do?" It was this group of letters that ultimately convinced me to write about what has happened in the past five years.

The Road to Freedom

I begin with humility and gratitude to God for breaking my addiction. I came to see the problem of lust as a true addiction, much like addiction to alcohol or drugs or gambling. And I can truly say that I have been set free of, in Augustine's words, "scratching lust's itchy sore." For those still caught in the web of that addiction, I bring a message of hope.

Ironically, I am most grateful for two things I normally try to avoid: guilt and fear. Augustine records rather candidly that, except for the fear of God's judgment in the afterlife, Epicurus would surely have lured him even deeper into carnal pleasures. A similar kind of fear and guilt kept me on edge during my long struggle with lust.

Psychologists use the term "cognitive dissonance" to describe the battle inside a person who believes one way and acts another. For example, a woman will normally feel intense cognitive dissonance if she secretly carries on an affair with another man while pretending to be happily married to her husband. Even if her husband suspects nothing, her own mind will constantly remind her that she is living with contradictions. Because the mind cannot sustain too much cognitive dissonance, it will seek ways to resolve the contradictions. Perhaps the wife will unconsciously let slip certain clues about her affair, or maybe she will accidentally call her husband by her lover's name. In such unexpected ways the mind will attempt to bring together her two lives.

A sense of cognitive dissonance haunted me during my addiction to lust. I believed one set of things about Christian ethics, the dangers of separating physical appeal from other aspects of sexuality, and the irrationality of an obsession with body parts. But I acted contrarily. From the pulpit I preached that a person's worth is measured internally, and that ugly people and fat people and the physically handicapped can express God's image. But, like much of male America, I spent my time drooling over shapely women with well-formed legs.

Most urgently, I experienced cognitive dissonance in my marriage. I had roped off large areas of my sexuality from my wife, which I cultivated in private, usually on trips, in visits to adult movie theaters and magazine shops. How could I expect to find sexual fulfillment in my marriage when I was nurturing a secret life of sexuality apart from my marriage?

Guilt and fear finally forced me to deal with the cognitive dissonance. Guilt made it feel dissonant in the first place; it constantly reminded me that my actions did not coincide with my beliefs. And fear, especially the fear I experienced after I learned how sex had utterly destroyed my Southern pastor friend, forced me to face my own sin. It led me, kicking and protesting all the way, toward repentance.

I mention this because guilt and fear do not often get good press in our liberated society. Had I sought help from a professional counselor, that counselor may well have dealt with the symptoms of guilt and fear rather than with the root problem. I have come to believe that the guilt and fear were wholly appropriate; they were, in fact, the prods that led me to resolve the cognitive dissonance in my life.

Today, I hear cries of outrage against anyone who, like former President Reagan or Jerry Falwell, conveys a tone of judgment. President Reagan simply asked that sexual abstinence be taught as an option, possibly the best option, for young people who wish to avoid the health dangers associated with sexual promiscuity. "Don't lay a guilt trip on us!" many people responded. "Don't try to scare us." But I have learned that guilt and fear may serve us well, as warnings against the direct dangers posed by a disease like AIDS, or against the more subtle dangers represented by an addiction to lust.

Yet guilt and fear are such powerful forces that they may also deceive. In my case, they deceived me into seeing God as my enemy. Now as I read "The War Within," it reminds me of a testimony delivered at a revival tent meeting: "For many years I wallowed in the stench and filth of sin until finally I reached the end of my rope and in desperation turned to God." Typically, as I did in the article, the testifier spends most of his time on vivid descriptions of the smells and sights of that sin.

I now view my pilgrimage differently. I believe God was with me at each stage of my struggle with lust. It wasn't that I had to climb toward a state of repentance to earn God's approval; that would be a religion of works. Rather, God was present with me even as I fled from him. At the moment when I was most aware of my own inadequacy and failure, at that moment I was probably closest to God. That is a religion of grace.

The title of one book on my shelf, *He Came Down from Heaven*, summarizes the gospel pretty well. Immanuel: God is with us, no matter what. He calls us to heaven but descends to earth to rescue us.

I wish we in the church did a better job of conveying God's love for sinners. From the church, I feel mainly judgment. I cannot bring my sin to the church until it has been neatly resolved into a warm, uplifting testimony. For example, if I had come to the church in the midst of my addiction to lust, I would have been harshly judged. That, in fact, is why I had to write my article anonymously. Even after the complete cycle of confession and forgiveness, people still wrote in comments like, "The author cannot possibly be considered a Christian."

Having said that, however, I also recognize that many people who struggle with addictions have been greatly helped by counselors or other mature Christians to whom they have made themselves accountable. They testify that knowing there is someone to whom they have to report honestly and regularly has been a key factor in resisting temptation.

I have attended a few meetings of Alcoholics Anonymous, and they convinced me that we in the church have something to learn from that group. Somehow they require accountability *and* communicate the "Immanuel-ness" of God. He is with you when you succeed and when you fail. He does not wait with folded arms for you to pick yourself out of the gutter. His hands are stretched out toward you, eager to help. Where are the hands of the church?

Bearing Scars

So far I have given mostly good news: the good news that an addiction can be broken, that God's love extends to the uttermost, that even guilt and fear can work for our good. But in honesty I must bring bad news as well.

In Sunday school we learn simple illustrations about the long-term effects of sin: "God will forgive you for the sin of smoking, but you'll always have spots on your lungs." Damage from sexual sins is rarely so easy to detect, but such sins do indeed have consequences.

I bear scars from my addiction to lust, even though the addiction seems broken. First, there is the scar of "spoiled innocence." Sex has a certain "you can't go back again" quality. Pornographers understand this well: They know that what titillates this month will only bore next month, and they must constantly search for new and exciting sexual variety in order to hold a viewer's attention. Pornography feeds on our fascination with the forbidden, but as the rules of what is forbidden change, our fascination changes as well. We want more.

I don't know exactly how to describe this long-term effect, but I definitely feel a sense of spoiled innocence. My sexual fantasy life far outstripped my sexual experience within marriage, and I have not been able to bring the two together. I was a voyeur, experiencing sex in loneliness and isolation. But sex is meant to be shared. To the degree that I indulged my voyeurism, I drifted away from my wife and our shared experiences.

And of course my years of deception undermined trust. Eventually, I told my wife everything about my addiction to lust, and she accepted it with astonishing grace and forgiveness. Still, though, she must wonder: When he travels alone, is he trustworthy? I sometimes wonder if I can even trust myself. By living in a state of cognitive dissonance for a number of years, I developed a great ability to live falsely. As I ignored the early warning signs of guilt, I opened up even greater possibilities for self-deception. Perhaps I have seared my own conscience. I continue to pray for the Holy Spirit's healing of my receptivity to him.

These are some of the long-term effects from my experience with lust. Surely similar scars form as a result of adultery, divorce, or a decision to abort a child. God will forgive such actions and grant repentance and restoration. But healing does not come free of long-term cost.

How do I respond to sexual pressures now? I am still a sexual being, a male. That has not changed. I still experience the same magnetic force of sexual desire that used to pull me toward pornography. What do I do with those urges? What do any of us do? As I see it, we can respond in three possible ways: indulgence, repression, or reconnection.

The Way of Indulgence

"The War Within" described in detail — some say too much detail — a process of indulgence, of following my sexual desires wherever they might lead. Our society seems strangely schizophrenic on the wisdom of that approach. On the one hand, authors advocating "The New Celibacy" appear on talk shows, and *Time* features articles on the new ethic of intimacy. On the other hand, you need only flip through the advertisements in a magazine like *Vogue* or *Glamour* to realize our society's approving attitude toward lust.

"Lust is back!" heralded an article in *Esquire* a few years ago. The sexual revolution of the sixties stemmed from an overall assault against tradition and authority. Soon feminism put a damper on anything that treated women as sexual objects. But now it seems perfectly acceptable to treat either women or men as sexual objects. Today's sexual revolution is fueled not so much by a reaction against authority as by The New Paganism that glorifies the human body (witness the incredible boom in body-building, fitness, and exercise).

Cable television and videocassettes now make pornography available to nearly everyone. The recent book *Vital Signs* reports that of Christian households hooked into cable television, 23 percent subscribe to porno channels — the same percentage as the nation as a whole.

What harm is there, after all, in displaying a little skin? Christians tend to be so uptight about sex; why not experiment with pornography to help loosen us up? There are many answers, I suppose, but one especially seems to fit my experience: pornography radically disconnects sex from its intended meaning. Human sexuality, a gift from God, was designed to express a relationship between a man and a woman, but pornography separates out one aspect of that gift — physical appeal — and focuses exclusively on it.

The specialists like to remind us that sexuality reveals our animal nature. It is a matter of biology, they say, of glands and hormones and physical maturation. Sex is technique: it can be learned, and mastered, and perfected. And perhaps pornography can assist you in mastering the technique.

But certain facts about human sexuality still puzzle the experts. While it resembles animal sexuality in some ways, it also expresses fundamental differences. Human beings possess disproportionate sexual equipment: among mammals, only human females develop enlarged breasts before their first pregnancy, and among primates the human male has the largest penis. In contrast to virtually all other animals, human beings engage in sex as a year-round option rather than limiting intercourse to the time of estrus. Behaviorists puzzle over these anomalies. What evolutionary advantage do they offer?

Perhaps the answer does not lie in "evolutionary advantage" at all. Perhaps it lies in the nature of human sexuality as an expression of relationship rather than as an act of instinct for the purpose of reproduction.

The most telling difference between human and animal sexuality is this: all other animals perform sexual acts in the open, without embarrassment. Only human beings see any advantage to privacy. "Man is the only animal that blushes, or needs to," said Mark Twain. For us, sex is different. It has an aura of mystery about it, and instinctively we want to keep it separate, to experience it in private. We treat it as we treat religion, with an aura of apartness, or "holiness."

As free creatures, human beings can, of course, rebel against these natural tendencies that have characterized all human societies. We can treat sex as an animal function, separating out the physical act from any aspect of relationship. We can tear down all the fences that societies have traditionally erected to protect the mystery surrounding sexuality. That, in fact, is precisely what pornography does. And it does so at our peril.

A few years ago in major cities like San Francisco, you could find certain establishments that catered to the sexual interests of gay men. Some of these reduced sex to its most base nature. A man could enter a stall and insert his genitals through an opening in the wall at crotch level. He could thus have a sex act performed on him without ever seeing his sexual partner. Such parlors offered efficient and anonymous sex, free from the trammels of relationship. In 1970, at the height of the gay sexual revolution, Kinsey Institute researchers found that 40 percent of white male homosexuals in San Francisco had had at least 500 sexual partners and 28 percent reported over 1,000 partners. (The hysteria over AIDS has greatly reduced those statistics, although now "safe sex" is being touted as a way to enjoy such pleasures without the risk of infection.)

What does all this frenetic sexual activity prove? It demonstrates, of course, the enormous power of the sexual drive in human beings, who are capable of indulgence at a rate without precedent in the animal kingdom. And it also shows that sex can be reduced to an utterly anonymous act, disconnected from relationship. The San Francisco statistics make that point most dramatically, but our society offers many other, more subtle reminders. "What's love got to do with it?" Tina Turner bellows into a microphone. Surely you can have great sex without the complications of love.

As I look back over the lessons I have learned, this seems the most important. Lust, and its expression in pornography, led me away from relationship toward raw desire. It enticed me with the promise of relationship: Cheryl Tiegs and Madonna and the monthly Playmates would remove their clothes and smile at me from the pages of magazines. But the photos lied. I was developing a relationship with ink dots printed on paper, not with real human beings.

Gradually, at a deep level, I was learning to view sex as mere technique, an exercise like gourmet dining. I was forgetting the crucial distinction between gourmet dining and gourmet sex: I have no human relationship with the food I eat, but I must have some sort of relationship with a sexual partner. Pornography attempts to abolish that distinction.

The magazines, especially the soft porno magazines, convey the message that sex is merely a physical act, a matter of technique. Television soap operas, in their own way, express much the same thing: only 6 percent of the sex depicted on them occurs between a husband and wife. Through them, we learn that we can disconnect the sex act from normal social mores.

And yet society can never sever the connections completely. Inconsistencies continue to surface. Consider two examples:

— Every society on earth acknowledges incest taboos. The United States, if anything, has recently become even more sensitive to incest and sexual abuse of children. But why? If sex is merely a physical act, a matter of technique, what difference should it make if parent and child have sex together, or brother and sister? The taboo against incest shows that human relationships are a part of sex at its most basic level.

— Movies very often depict an affair that begins "just on a physical basis." But rarely can the characters continue the affair on that basis. It grows, dominating the characters' emotions and gradually undermining their marriages. The old cycle of cognitive dissonance sets in, and what began as a physical affair soon blossoms into a full-fledged relationship. Linda Wolfe, a feminist author, wrote a book called *Playing Around: Women and Extramarital Sex*, in which she expressed amazement that so many physical affairs begun "to preserve a marriage by giving me a sexual outlet" ended up destroying that marriage.

I have come to realize that the greatest danger of pornography lies in its false depiction of sexuality. It focuses exclusively on physical appearance and technique, without recognizing sex as an expression of relationship between two human beings. Because pornography begins with a false premise, the more I follow where it leads, the less able I will be to find a well-integrated, healthy experience of sexuality.

Gay men in San Francisco with 1,000 partners may be light years beyond me in sexual technique and proficiency. But I doubt whether they have found a high level of mature sexual satisfaction. They have addressed the "animal" aspect of their sexuality, but at the expense of developing relationships. We are more than animals: that is the basic Christian contribution to sexuality. (And, in fact, as the anomalies of human sexuality show — disproportionate sexual organ size, the need for privacy, the constant availability — in sexuality we may be *least* like other animals.) Whatever leads me to emphasize exclusively the "animal" side of my sexuality will likely lead toward confusion and dissatisfaction.

I have learned that my addiction to lust probably expressed other human needs. What was I searching for in the porno literature and movies? The image of the perfect female breast?

More likely, I was searching for intimacy, or love, or acceptance, or reinforcement of an insecure male ego, or maybe even a thirst for transcendence. I was searching for something that could never be satisfied by two-dimensional photos printed on slick magazine paper. And not until I recognized that could I begin to turn toward a more appropriate sexual identity.

In my search, I "de-mystified" sexuality. I made the female body as common as a daily newspaper, rather than as rare as the one woman I had chosen to spend my life with. I destroyed the fences around sexuality, chasing away any remnants of "holiness." Nudity became not the final mutual achievement in a progression toward intimacy, but the very first step. These are the results of my choices toward indulgence. From all of them, I am still trying to recover.

The Temptation of Repression

Some people writing in response to my original LEADERSHIP article could not identify with my struggle at all. They offered me stern advice, mostly consisting of admonishments from the Bible.

Wrote one pastor: "Nowhere does the Bible say to pray for victory over lust. It does say to flee immorality (1 Cor. 6:18). It does say to saturate our minds with Scripture (Ps. 119:9, 11). It does say to make a covenant with our eyes so that we do not gaze on a virgin (Job 31:1). It does say to take every thought captive to Christ (2 Cor. 10:3-5)."

Several people also cited the apostle Paul's statement about the perversions of Ephesus, "It is disgraceful even to speak of the things which are done by them in secret."

Reading so many of these letters in one sitting, I had to question my own experience. In my struggles with lust, was I making complex something that should have been simple? I had written page after page about "the war within" and the forces that pulled me toward lust. The letter writers seemed to think the solution to lust was the same as the solution to the drug problem in America: Just Say No!

But then I read the letters of people who had felt every moment of my struggle. These, among them godly men and women, had succumbed to temptation. A firm resolution to say no did not seem enough.

What is the difference between "fleeing immorality" and simple repression? By automatically turning away from any impulse toward sexual desire, will I dam up a reservoir of repression that will one day overflow? I don't know, but I do believe that we who learn to practice repression at an early age may be woefully unprepared to face real temptation.

I think of the classical distinction between virtue and innocence: virtue, unlike innocence, has successfully passed a point of temptation. Perhaps a person who grows up in a Christian subculture, attends Christian schools, watches Christian television, reads Christian books, and listens to Christian music can survive these days in something like a state of innocence. But there is a danger also: a person reared in such a hothouse environment may wilt once he or she steps into the broader society.

I grew up in a sheltered Christian background, where I learned to rely on simple, black-and-white, just-say-no repression as the best defense against all forms of temptation. But that defense failed me in the matter of lust. I was utterly unprepared for the force, the almost magical force, of human sexuality.

Since those days of innocence, I have read thinkers like Wilhelm Reich, Arthur Schopenhauer, and Sigmund Freud, each of whom explains almost all human behavior on the basis of the sexual instinct. I do not agree with them, but they do underscore the enormous power of human sexuality.

"I feel as if I have escaped from the hands of a mad and furious master," said Sophocles when old age finally quelled his sexual drive. Sex cannot be reduced to neat, rational formulas and explained away. And I wonder whether any degree of repression can withstand its force. Will any amount of repression ever prepare us for virtue?

Yet I must confess that in the past five years, I have often used pure repression as a response to temptation. Once the back of my "addiction" to lust had been broken, I was able to repress temptations in that direction. But just saying no became possible only after I had dealt with the nature of the lust impulse.

Different people develop different ways of controlling their sexual impulses. I recently read of the French Thomist philosopher Jacques Maritain, who together with his wife took a vow of celibacy. Both in their early thirties and having been married ten years, they kept the vow the rest of their lives. Maritain revealed his secret only after Raissa's death: "We decided to renounce a thing which marriage fulfills, a deep need of the human being — both of body and spirit. . . . I do not say that any such decision was easy to take. . . . It implied no scorn for nature but a desire to follow at any price at least one of the counsels of the perfect life." Maritain also reported that "one of the great graces of our life was that . . . our mutual love was infinitely increased." I stand in awe before such a decision, even as I choose another way for myself. But whatever you think about the Maritains' choice, it hardly seems like repression. They made the choice in full awareness of their sexuality, in full commitment to their relationship. It sounds more like virtue than like innocence.

I ultimately came to reject repression as the best response to my sexuality for the same reason that I rejected indulgence: it fails to satisfy the underlying human needs. Indulgence meets temporary needs but disconnects them from the underlying needs of intimacy. Similarly, repression may give me an escape from an immediate temptation toward lust, but it will not satisfy the state that made me susceptible to lust in the first place.

Reconnecting the Sexual Self

The only ultimate solution for my sexual needs, I am convinced, will involve finding a balanced and mature way of expressing the full range of my sexuality within my marriage. I experienced sex in its "disconnected" form, as a voyeur of other people's bodies, apart from a relationship. My healing process will surely involve reconnecting that sexual power and energy with the growth toward intimacy it was designed to accompany.

G. K. Chesterton once likened this world to the desert island site of a shipwreck. A sailor awakes from a deep sleep and discovers treasure strewn about, relics from a civilization he can barely remember. One by one he picks up the relics — gold coins, a compass, fine clothing — and tries to discern their meaning. According to Chesterton, fallen humanity is in such a state. Good things on earth still bear traces of their original purpose, but each is also subject to misinterpretation or abuse because of fallen, "amnesiac" human nature.

Evil is a kind of subverted echo of goodness and spirituality. Power, a wonderful human gift, can be used for great good or can through violence be used to dominate others. Wealth may lead to charity or to exploitation; delicious food may inspire gratitude or gluttony.

Sexual desire, one of the most powerful "relics" we find on this earth, invites obsession. When we experience sexual desires, it seems only right to follow where they lead. As the modern song puts it, "It can't be wrong when it feels so right."

John J. McNeill, the Jesuit psychotherapist who was expelled from his order for his teachings in his ministry to gay people, wrote, "I was convinced that what is bad psychologically has to be bad theologically and that, conversely, whatever is good theologically is certainly good psychologically." McNeill then concluded, "Every human being has a God-given right to sexual love and intimacy."

McNeill's philosophy sounds very appealing. Who could argue against our psychological good corresponding to our theological good? His philosophy has only one basic problem: If I am the one determining my psychological good, there will be no end to my rationalization. A bulimic teenager may, for example, determine that vomiting will make her feel better psychologically, and thus starve herself to death. An alcoholic may determine that one more pint of Scotch would provide oh so much psychological relief.

The problem is that *we* are the problem. The good things on earth — food, drink, sex, recognition, power, wealth — are not spoiled; we are. They are relics of Eden. But our amnesia affects our very ability to determine their proper use.

Christians, of course, believe that we have a message from the one who designed the relics, the ship, and the sailor. That message teaches us that sex is tied to relationship, and desire finds its best and most satisfying fulfillment within marriage. It's a message I do not always like, and one I have often rebelled against. But I am convinced it is true. And thus the only hope for me to find balance and maturity in my sex life is to pray and work toward a healthy marriage relationship, which includes sex.

The authors of the best-selling book *Habits of the Heart* reported that, of all the people they interviewed, only evangelical Christians were able to articulate a reason for continuing to believe in marriage. We have been given a message from God that connects and gives meaning to such things as physical desire, gender differences, reproduction, love, and mutual sacrifice.

I now see the challenge before me as a process of reconnecting what, during my addiction to lust, I had so tragically separated. Can my physical desire for my wife develop along with my desire for union with her emotionally, and even spiritually? Can our experience of union, interpenetration, and shared pleasure convey the very deep spiritual — more, sacramental — significance that lies at the heart of a Christian view of marriage?

I would like to conclude with a glowing profile of how that has been accomplished in my marriage. I cannot, not yet. My wife and I are both committed to that goal, and we both seek it. We will continue to seek it even as we recover from the distrust and distance that entered our lives during my addiction to lust.

Easy Lie or Hard Truth

I tremble to say this in an age when anyone who focuses on the differences between the sexes is held up to ridicule, but I am convinced that the experience of lust is one in which gender differences stand out strongest. The same Kinsey Institute survey that discovered almost half the male homosexuals in San Francisco had more than 500 partners also revealed that more than half the gay white women surveyed had had less than ten sexual partners. Most of those women rarely had casual sex and tended toward monogamy with one gay partner.

The striking difference in statistics might shed light on this whole issue of lust. Wives wrote to me confessing that my article had touched on an area of great conflict in their marriages. When their husbands had admitted some acquaintance with pornography, the wives found that disgusting and perverted.

I would not attempt a theory on why sexual aggression and lust seem more of a danger to men than to women. But the picture comes clear if you simply compare the number of porno magazines directed toward men with those directed toward women. Or, simply stand outside an adult movie theater and count the number of men and women who enter. The compulsive thirst for sexuality that leads to the voyeurism seems to fall more within the male domain. It contains within it an element of sexual aggression that seems foreign to most women.

What does a man want in sex? What need was being met in the days when I would fawn over photos of women I would never meet? What lay behind the appeal? Pastors' wives wrote to ask me the question, and in turn I have asked it of myself.

Here is the answer that seems closest to me. In sex, I want to feel welcome. I want to feel accepted, not rejected. In some primal sense, I want to feel like a conquering king, like a warrior (and I know how out of fashion those images are in this liberated age).

Yet, ironically, sex combines aggression and insecurity in a precarious balance. I think most women would be surprised to learn how intimidating, even terrifying, sex is for many men. Pornography lowers the terror. It's an easy form of arousal. And the key to the arousal is the illusion of welcomeness. Miss October arches her back and spreads her legs. Beautiful women from around the globe smile at me, beckon me to enjoy them.

Real life is never so easy. Sex comes, for most of us, after months or years of courtship. There is romance, yes, but there is also conflict, boredom, and incompatibility. The woman I desire is busy asserting herself, seeking her identity, fending off a culture that tends to treat her like a sex object. She has kids around the house, a career to juggle with her other chores, and financial hassles. Unlike Miss October, she doesn't spend all day preparing herself to look appealing and available.

So I am left with an easy lie or a hard truth. The easy lie is the illusion of pornography. It offers its own rewards, and I would be dishonest if I said its appeal eventually vanishes. It doesn't. I miss the thrill that lust used to provide me, just as a recovered drug addict misses the highs he once experienced. How can sex in marriage, complicated by real-life commitments, intricacies of compatibility, and the inconveniences of children, possibly compete with the illusory thrills of *Playboy* women?

But there is a hard truth suggested by Chesterton's analogy of the shipwreck. Why are we here? Are we on earth primarily to experience pleasure, to have fun? If so, Christianity, with its offer of a cross and sacrificial love and concern for the weak and the poor, seems pretty thin. If we are here for no real reason, why go through all the bother of trying to connect glandular desire with lofty goals like intimacy and marriage?

Or are we here on a mission? Are we indeed creatures who will best find fulfillment by living up to the demands of the Creator? If the latter, then the thrills offered by the easy lie of pornography will not permanently satisfy. Indulgence is not an option for me, and neither is repression. I have only one option: to seek God with all my heart, so that God may continue his process of healing and bring me to sexual fulfillment — at home, with my wife, where I belong.

FOUR

AFTER THE AFFAIR: A WIFE'S STORY

Why would a highly thought of "man of God" risk — no, throw away — all he has worked so hard for, just to try to satisfy emotional "needs"?

HEATHER BRYCE

he phone rang. It was late in the afternoon, the day after Christmas. "I'm coming from the church office to get you," Bill said. "Meet me outside. I'll be right there."

His voice sounded heavy. *What could be so wrong?* I wondered. I hurriedly put on my boots and coat, and then stepped outside and stood in the cold to wait.

Bill pulled into the driveway. "What's wrong?" I asked as I climbed into the car.

"The worst."

"What?"

He looked at me. "Promise me you'll believe I love you. Will you promise me that?"

"Well, of course. Why?"

We drove into the church parking lot and came to a stop. He took my hand and told me that Ron Kelton (the new pastor of our former church) and the district superintendent were inside. "They have signed statements charging me with inappropriate behavior and immoral actions."

"Bill, they must be mistaken!" I said. "Someone is lying about you. Or somebody didn't understand what he saw." I looked at him. "They are wrong, aren't they?"

"The charges are exaggerated," he said, "but one is undeniable."

"Who?"

"Kate." He looked down.

The full impact of what this would mean still didn't hit me. We walked into Bill's study, and I greeted the two sober-faced men.

"Has Bill informed you of the charges against him?" they asked me as gently as they could when we were seated. I reached for Bill's hand and repeated what he had told me in the car. They began explaining the situation as they knew it. Bill would not defend himself; he had already been talking with them for three hours. I tried to defend him. I knew Bill — surely he couldn't be guilty of this. Much of the evidence was only circumstantial, after all. But they blocked my every argument with facts.

The men said that even with his confession and repentance, he would not be able to stay in the pulpit. I couldn't see why. If he went to God for forgiveness, why did he have to throw away years of much-appreciated hard work?

Then I felt chilled: *It did happen, and there is no way out.* Soon, if not immediately, my husband would have no ministry — maybe anywhere, ever. We would have to leave our parsonage and our church family. All security was gone.

"Are you willing to stay with him?" the district superintendent asked me.

"Yes," I said. Though still in shock, I knew I loved him. And besides, where else would I go?

"Since Bill has declared that he loves you, and you want to stay with him," they said, "we feel the next step is for you to spend some time at a retreat and counseling center in Tennessee." During our two weeks there, we were to be under the counseling care of a Christian psychologist. We could confront each other, face the facts, and determine directions for the future. The center had an opening in three days.

We drove home in silence. In the house waited our entire

family except for one son and his family who had not been able to come for Christmas.

When we walked in, they were already huddled together. They knew something was wrong by the way I had left suddenly — without explanation. When they saw our faces, they asked, "What's wrong? Someone complaining? A conflict in the church?"

Then Bill told them what I had just learned. They couldn't believe it. Stunned and in tears, they gathered around us and prayed for us.

The next two days, I moved in slow motion. It was hard to talk. Even lifting a fork took effort. I was glad for the needs of my little granddaughters. They still needed to be hugged and cared for, and in return, they loved me.

I wandered through our parsonage, trying to visualize packing and moving out. I couldn't. I couldn't cope with the thought.

At night, I began waking often. I'd try to understand my new situation. *I'm married to a man I don't know. I'm not a pastor's wife anymore.* When I'd wake up, Bill would get up, too, and hold me and rub my back while I sobbed.

That made me aware of the unending pain of those whose husbands leave for the other woman. I was grateful to God and to Bill that he wanted to stay. There were human arms to comfort and to confirm love, as well as the undergirding arms of the Father.

Making arrangements to be gone for two weeks required calling together the church board. We had been instructed not to tell them of our problem, but they couldn't avoid seeing the change in us. Each looked concerned, but we could not reassure them.

The morning we left for Tennessee, we tried to capture the feeling of going on vacation. We hadn't been able to take our vacation for nearly three years.

The first day on the road there were miles and miles of tears and talk. Through it, I grew better able to deal with the charges and the anger created by them. I could see where I had fallen short of meeting his needs to be close. The Lord brought to my mind many times I had been prompted to reach out to him, to make advances, to go and sit by him, even to sit on his lap. Usually, however, I would give in to continuing the busywork at hand. I determined to heed those promptings in the future.

That night at the motel, we walked in and sat down — Bill on the edge of one double bed and me on the other, facing each other. I knew he didn't feel free to reach out. I got up and went over and sat by him, and then cuddled next to him, to his apparent relief and delight.

The next day as we drove, Bill paused and said, "I think you need to know there's a couple more."

"No! Who?"

"Rose. And Helen."

Friends, close friends of mine for years! Helen was as close to me as my sister. I wanted to get out of the car, to run, but couldn't. I threw my empty soda cup at him and then took off my rings and threw them at him, too. Then I pulled the collar of my sweater up over my face and cried.

Again, though, I knew I had to set aside rage and move toward understanding. Over the years I'd dealt with many who were angry or depressed, and I didn't want to stay in that self-centered state. I had to be able to see all the sides of this situation. Somehow.

We had to stop and call for directions to the retreat center and were instructed to get groceries before continuing to the chalet. I've never had such a hard time deciding between white and wheat bread.

When we arrived, I thought I already had the whole story. But it took six days of confrontation to extract all the facts. Through clever hedging and conscious lying, Bill had covered the extent of his immoral actions.

These are facts I still struggle with today: Fourteen years ago he was confronted by an attractive woman in our small church, who stated that she planned to leave the church because she was in love with him. Subsequently she invited him to join her at a motel where she had gone for "a day of seeking God's will." That affair lasted six months. They cut it off, knowing they were not meant to live together. She was my friend before, during, and after.

There were ten years free of involvement until one of the women who later signed a statement against Bill chased him until she caught him. I knew she was chasing, but I assumed he was running.

A few other involvements of varying degrees followed in a short period of time. He set them all aside for a year, and then we moved to another church.

In time he entered a low-level affair, which lasted three months until just prior to the confrontation.

All of these women were my friends.

I struggled with why it was such a battle for him to confess everything. He was relieved to have the impending nightmare of confrontation over. He was weary from fear, guilt, sleepless nights, depression, physical dissipation, and suicidal thoughts. (I had credited what I had seen to pastoral stress, and he let me believe that.) He could scarcely look me in the eye anymore or talk through anything. He wanted our relationship restored. He cared enough to stay and squarely face the consequences rather than run.

But still he could hardly make himself confess the extent of his immoral acts.

I finally understood that his reticence did make some sense. In telling the truth, he was destroying his own self-image — and the reputation of the women. He was destroying the faith placed in him by his peers, his trusting congregations, his family. He couldn't know if I would be able to withstand the pain and fear, or if in losing my trust and respect for him I could ever continue to love him. He recoiled from having to hear my anguish and see my rage. He also had to bear his own pain and guilt *out loud*.

In holding back facts for all of these reasons, however important to him, he nonetheless perpetuated deceit. He removed much of what was left of his integrity and, except for the Lord's grace, made the rebuilding of trust with me nearly impossible. He was trying to operate from a false sense of valor —"I'll bear it myself; what's not known hurts no one but me." To me, that was like carrying water in a bucket full of holes.

All had to be bared, exposed to the light, in order for healing and trust to begin. Since God's forgiveness follows true repentance after full confession, there would be no hope for the future until every involvement, like a deeply buried tendril, was uprooted. Only then could the sin wither and die.

God's Word instructs us to forgive one another. Since not to forgive is also sin, I had no choice but to forgive. And so I did, not just my husband but all participants. Noble? No! There is simply no choice.

Being wronged is miserable, but doing the wrong exacts a greater toll in every way. It is a lighter burden to be the forgiver than the one being forgiven, but at first it felt as if I, the wronged one, had no rights. I was supposed to just bear it, forgive it, and go on.

To be fair, at the retreat center we came to relish the unending, uninterrupted time together. We enjoyed leisure and hours of honeymooning, even though interspersed with torrents of tears and ranting rages.

As our stay drew to an end, I was full of feelings and thoughts of what happened. We wanted to stay — until the groceries were gone, until the snow melted — anything to postpone going back home to the loss of our church. But we finally left that place of storming rage and hesitant, but beginning, forgiveness.

Driving by the church, turning into the driveway, and stopping in the garage didn't produce the usual "It's good to be home" feelings. Facing us were weeks of trial.

Bill began writing letters of confession and resignation for all the offices he held. He wrote a letter to the former church board and the present one. The district superintendent asked him to declare publicly his confession and resignation in a church service. He did.

The next week we went to our former church. At the close of the evening service, we were ushered to a pew near the front, surrounded by elders who were also close friends. That church had been built with many hard years of what I thought had been dedicated labor. We could scarcely walk the aisle.

After several statements by those in charge, Bill was called to the pulpit. He managed to state that to his sorrow and shame he had experienced repeated moral failure and asked for the forgiveness of the church people, present pastor, and me. An elder sat on each side of me, squeezing my hands. I struggled not to sob openly.

At the end of the service, the pastor invited those who wanted to set aside the sin in their lives to come to the altar for prayer. As people responded, he invited some altar workers to come also and pray for the others. One of the altar workers he asked was the "attractive woman" of fourteen years ago!

My mind was screaming. I pressed my hands over my mouth to keep from saying anything.

While people prayed, dozens of others came to us to express their love and concern. Eventually this woman, my friend of twenty years, approached me.

Rather than let her touch me, I reached out and held her by the arm. Looking her in the eye, I said softly, "Helen, I forgive you."

She didn't flinch but said, "But nobody knows!"

Does she crumple and cry, "I'm so sorry for what I did! I, too, am devastated by your pain and loss"? No, she's so in control with her "But no one knows!"

I could only reply, "You opened the door, Helen." I turned and walked over to where my husband was standing and watched her as she left the church. I wanted to scream and point her out. I wanted to scratch her face to ribbons. Somehow, God enabled me to keep my peace.

These things torture, but remarkably, with time, love and forgiveness do flow back. Even though old hurts can be stirred, a measure of healing begins.

Forgetting, though, takes much more time.

Several concerned individuals donated money for us to spend time at another counseling retreat in Colorado. Again, conflicts were isolated and communication needs examined.

Again we returned to the "real world." Bill was full of apprehension about a job and our financial situation. Pastors don't receive unemployment, and paychecks cease. And no entry-level job can replace the salary of a senior pastor after twenty-five years of ministry. He finally took a job in sales.

I was trying to understand some of the "why." Even today I am confused by nebulous terms such as *need, isolation, lonely, closed, and open.* These needed to be defined and worked through in our relationship.

The Persistent Question

What causes a highly regarded "man of God" to risk — no, throw away — all he has worked so hard for just to try to satisfy emotional "needs"?

The bottom line, of course, is not a "what" but "who." Satan, the enemy of the godly, manages to deceive a person into believing his needs (self) are first and foremost. The very human pastor with his own needs and weaknesses is in a battle against unseen principalities and powers.

There are unique pressures within ministries, though, that contribute to losing the battle.

Insufficient income is demeaning and apt to cause strife at home. It can plant doubt about God's sufficiency and care. It can cause the wife to seek outside work, leading to a feeling of distance.

For the most part, *first churches or fledgling ministries are demanding* to the extreme. While a young family grows, all the couple's strength and energy are expended. Improper priorities and poor communication habits can start. These are subtle, seem normal, and go unnoticed.

Undefined success in ministry causes further problems. A pastor, like anyone, needs to feel he is succeeding. Success in the ministry should not be measured by human standards, but it is. A pastor is always, and especially at midlife, battling to feel he has done well.

High expectations exact a toll. The job description for the pastorate may sound reasonable, but actual expectations probably aren't. An unspoken one in many churches is they are hiring a team; a pastor's wife is expected to fill in for any talent lacking. If she is not good at what she is asked to do, her husband is told in emphatic terms. If she is good, her time and energy go to other people or tasks rather than to him.

Another factor is *loneliness.* A pastor, like any leader, often feels isolated. He seldom has a safe person with whom to share his loneliness, or feelings of failure, or doubts that God is caring for him.

A pastor's wife, meanwhile, may face loneliness, depression, weariness, hurt, and fear. Her problems, to the extent they are caused by him, threaten him. Thus, she has no pastor to turn to. She knows her husband helps others freely, but she learns to find other means and people to meet her needs.

Then there is the *"professional license"* to keep secrets, which reflects itself in conversations like this:

"Who did you talk to today, Dear?"

"People with problems, as usual."

"Like who?"

"It is best you don't know, okay?"

In order not to spend all her time jealous, curious, or angry, a pastor's wife has to give her husband to his work — almost to the point of not caring.

The Widening Gap

I know the scenario that can develop in a pastoral marriage. Following a day with complaints and problems, a lonely, tired pastor comes home to a lonely, tired wife. He gives and gets the usual greeting.

The wife, usually getting supper, would enjoy a little help and talk. However, she knows her husband has only a short time before going to a committee meeting, Bible study, or hospital or home visit. He would like one half-hour to pursue his own activity. The wife thinks she is doing him a favor to give him space.

Many pastors and their wives get together only in the car on the way to or from an activity. Once inside the church, they go to their separate areas of service. Rarely do they sit together or pray together. When the service is over, they circulate in different areas so they can touch as many people as possible. At last, the lights are out, the doors are closed, and they are off — to have company, be company, or go with others for ice cream and fellowship. By the time they get home, all their sparkle is gone, their personalities flat. They fall into bed, exhaustion overriding any chance for intimacy.

As a result, both are lonely, needy, and vulnerable. Wives opt out, too, but pastors are faced with greater temptations. They are there to listen to hurting women. Many receive the insistent call, "Come to my house. I really need you!" When met at the door by an admiring woman inappropriately dressed, the chance to share dreams and hidden loneliness beckons strongly. One unguarded moment can set up a giddy, then unbearable, self-defeating, guilt-enveloping relationship, in the name of "meeting needs," both his and hers.

All he has to do to deceive his wife is say, "I had an appointment today." Simple.

The Price

But the price is great.

The average parishioner who falls need only come to the pastor's office with his or her spouse, confess, and receive forgiveness. The two are given support and go on with their lives. The situation is painful, but few know. The couple keep their jobs, home, and sense of community.

A pastor who confesses, on the other hand, usually loses his position and income and residence, and is forced to leave the very community that should be giving him emotional support. He will be asked to confess publicly. He must resign all hard-won places of honor with his peers and denomination.

The relationship with his wife, kept so-so through deceit, now has to go through many painful stages. He has lost any reason to be trusted.

The bewildered, stunned pastor's wife suffers losses in addition to her husband's. They will move, thus costing her contact with her friends, and she may well lose her husband. At the least, she has lost her pastor. She loses her self-worth from both the adulteries and from leaving the ministries where she received approval. Since few people understand the whole situation, she is isolated at her point of greatest need. When able to stay within the marriage relationship, her only companion is the one who acted to hurt her.

The Unfairness of Forgiveness

My past, once cherished, is gone. I loathe and am contaminated by it. Yet, for others, life seems to continue unchanged. The "other women" — ex-friends, Christians — do not seem to need to say they are sorry or ask forgiveness, and that leaves an empty sense of loss. Counselors told me not to get in touch with any of them, and so forgiveness had to be only from me and not returned.

The support we have received has been primarily for my husband. Many, many letters to both of us encourage me to forgive him, and assure him that good has come from his past ministry. Many times the help I get is in the form of "Have you lost any weight? How are you treating him now?"

However, God created us to survive in the midst of trial; his grace is sufficient. In pain his joy is made manifest.

I experienced some of that joy this summer. In the spring Bill wrote me a long letter (he expresses himself best that way) telling me of his love for me and his commitment to me. He asked if I would "remarry" him. He wanted to renew his marriage vows.

So on our twenty-eighth anniversary, we restated and renewed our vows to each other in the woods near our home. Officiating were our district superintendent, our local pastor, and the pastor with whom we've been in counseling. I made my gown and bouquet of flowers. Our sons and daughters and their families came from across the country to be with us. One daughter decorated our wedding cake and the other sang in the ceremony. Bill gave me a brand-new wedding ring. This time the words "for better or for worse" took on a new and deeper meaning.

Twenty-eight years after we began our marriage, we began again.

PART II

PASTORAL PRECAUTIONS

The pastoral struggle with sexual temptation is real—and undeniably powerful. Yet there is good news. Sexual temptation can be reduced by paying attention to three crucial areas.

Professional counseling ethics *are designed to help control feelings of sexual attraction that can enter any therapeutic relationship. These counseling dangers—usually centered around the psychological phenomenon called transference—are compounded for the minister. Counselees see ministers as not only counselors, but as spiritual guides who can safely avoid the danger of friendship turning into passion. Such is not always the case.*

In Chapter 5, "Transference: Loosening the Tie That Blinds," Archibald Hart warns ministers of the dangers of transference. As dean of Fuller Theological Seminary's School of Psychology in Pasadena, California, Hart has helped hundreds of divinity students and working pastors confront this knotty problem.

Understanding your personal psyche *is absolutely crucial to controlling sexual temptations. Ministers are not cold theologians with all the answers. On the contrary, they are usually warm people who care deeply about the hurts of church members. That's not all. Church members usually exaggerate, in their own minds, the warmth of the pastor. Pastors are trained to say warm, caring things. The gospel message is a love story. Pastors good at telling this story are, well, sexy. They make inviting sexual targets.*

Louis McBurney has a retreat center in the Colorado Rockies for pastoral couples with marriages in crisis. Many of these crises are sexually related. In Chapter 6, "Avoiding the Scarlet Letter," McBurney talks about the factors that make ministers susceptible—and what they can do to guard against it.

Finally, facts of time and circumstances *have turned many an innocent meeting between pastor and parishioner into the first step toward an affair. It need not happen. Many simple, commonsense precautions can help nip potentially disastrous situations before they blossom. Randy Alcorn, pastor of small group ministries at Good Shepherd Community Church in Gresham, Oregon, shares some of these that he has learned. He also details in Chapter 7, "Strategies to Keep from Falling," a mental checklist he uses to warn himself of the dangers he faces.*

FIVE

TRANSFERENCE: LOOSENING THE TIE THAT BLINDS

The basic attraction to others should not concern us. What we do with the attraction is what is important.

ARCHIBALD HART

If you were hungry for love, wouldn't it be nice to find someone who was well-educated, mannerly, articulate but also a good listener, respected in the community, occupationally powerful, yet unselfish, and willing to spend time alone with you for free?

Numbers of counselees think so. They come to a church office and find themselves in the presence of the kindest, most receptive, admirable, gentle, wise person they've met in a long time. The solution to their turmoil, they gradually realize, is not so much what the pastor is saying as the pastor himself.

In my classes for working clergy who are pursuing the D.Min. degree, I talk about this hazard, technically known as transference. (The client is projecting feelings and desires into the counseling relationship that belong somewhere else.) Each term the students write a paper on how the course has related to their situations. Every time, 20 to 25 percent of them report transference as a problem they have faced in their ministries.

Countertransference, the even more distressing corollary, is when the *counselor* projects into the mix feelings and desires that belong elsewhere.

The Problem

At the outset, let me stress that an intimate relationship between a pastor and a church member does not always involve physical sex. Although such relationships have the potential to become sexual, they may remain as emotional attachments for a long time.

"I've been lonely," wrote one pastor, "and I cannot communicate with my wife. She doesn't understand how I feel. All she wants to talk about are the kids and her mother. I want to explore ideas, thoughts, and feelings. So I began to spend time with a woman after we finished our counseling sessions. She understands me. I can share myself with her. I hope this doesn't go further — I'd hate to have to decide whether to leave my wife or not."

This pastor is kidding himself. The relationship will go further if he does nothing to stop it. All sexual affairs begin in this benign way.

Although most liaisons emerge out of counseling relationships, some start when a minister has to work closely with someone on a committee or project. Since more and more younger women have assumed church responsibilities in recent years, male ministers are now in closer working relationships with women where feelings of warmth and affection can easily arise. Sometimes the relationship develops with a secretary or other work colleague.

Male pastors are typically attracted to younger women, although it is not unusual for ministers to be attracted to older ones as well. And attraction does not require extensive contact. Glances from the pulpit to someone hardly known, or a chance encounter in a corridor or on a hospital visit can find the pastor obsessed with a strong attraction to someone else.

Sexual responsiveness is fundamentally instinctive, even though it is heavily influenced by factors of learning. It is based in biology, with hormones that can powerfully control behavior and emotions. So the basic attraction to others should not concern us. It is quite normal.

What we do with the attraction is what is important. Whether we succumb to it, deny or repress it (which is often the gateway to a state of increased vulnerability at a later stage), or honestly and courageously confront and deal with the attraction will be determined not only by our spiritual maturity but also by our level of self-understanding and the professional competence derived from good training.

The apostle Paul, in 1 Thessalonians 4:3–5, says, "It is God's will that you should be holy; that you should avoid sexual immorality; that each of you should learn to control his own body in a way that is holy and honorable, not in passionate lust like the heathen, who do not know God."

In essence, Paul is telling us to understand our bodies and know how to control our urges and drives. Since much attraction gets out of hand in avoidable situations and arises out of needs the average pastor does not understand, better training about the counseling process can prevent the catastrophe of ministerial affairs.

How Transference Happens

I believe the main source of church-related sexual affairs is the counseling relationship.

Over the past decade, the topic of sexual intimacies with clients has received considerable attention in the helping professions. In California it is now illegal (not just unethical) for a psychotherapist to have sex with a client, even if evidence shows the client was the primary seducer and a willing participant. Psychotherapists are required to report all cases of clients who have had sexual encounters with previous psychotherapists.

These professions readily acknowledge that in the close, personal relationship of psychotherapy, warm, friendly, intimate feelings are bound to develop. Just as surgery produces blood, therapy produces a closeness that can easily be mislabeled "love." The competent therapist recognizes these feelings as a by-product of therapy and is trained to deal with them. His or her own hang-ups and unmet needs are not allowed to enter the picture.

True, not all psychotherapists are adequately trained or follow their training. But some ministers are not even aware of these issues, let alone have any training in dealing with them. Both need help.

Although a minister's personal family and married life is a basic deterrent to deliberately searching for an illicit affair, it does not guarantee safety in the counseling room or the more subtle encounters of committee or project work. I have always believed, despite protests from unsuspecting pastors, that a minister's vulnerability has nothing to do with his marital happiness. For many centuries Scripture has warned us to be on guard when we feel most safe! Sexual attraction can occur as easily when one is happily married as when one is not. You may more deliberately *seek out* an affair when you are not happy, but you are not necessarily safe when all is bliss at home.

Contributing Factors

All ministers are vulnerable to affairs for the following reasons:

• *The counseling relationship* provides an opportunity to explore the feelings of another person. People not involved in counseling don't get the same opportunity and probably can't grasp how deeply satisfying a true empathic understanding can be.

I know some ministers who deliberately do not do one-to-one counseling; they want to avoid the closeness either because they perceive themselves as too needful of intimacy or because they are physically very attractive to the opposite sex and constantly have to fight off their advances. This is a sensible decision in these cases.

• *The pastoral image.* Male ministers can be very attractive to women simply because of their role. They are perceived as caring, concerned, and helping, yet with a power that is exciting. They can attract pretty women who in other settings would not give them a second look. Many ministers confuse this attraction to their role with attraction to their person.

They are also perceived as "safe." Intimate experiences with ministers do not typically create as much guilt in women as would other affairs: "After all, if the pastor is willing, it can't be that bad." Many are misled into believing they can allow their warm, loving feelings to develop with a minister because he will know where and when to set the limits. When they find that no such limits are set, they often panic. In other words, the minister, having stepped out of his role, is no longer seen as attractive; he has destroyed the very reason for his attractiveness. He suddenly finds himself facing an accuser.

● *The denial of sexual urges*. It is an unfortunate consequence of our Christian aspirations to holiness that we create a sexually repressive subculture. Many ministers (and Christians in general) are afraid of their sexuality and see in it a tremendous potential for sin. And they are right. The healthier way to deal with the sex drive is to bring it into the open and courageously confront and master it.

The majority of ministers enter their profession with the highest ethical intentions. They have a deep desire to be genuine and spiritual. But often they also are confused about their sexuality, and rather than confronting their feelings, they repress or deny them. Believing they are immune to sexual temptations, and often denying the emotions that are staring them in the face, they increase their vulnerability. When the inevitable finally happens, everyone is shocked. But they have marched headlong into trouble, their traditional role and high moral standards fortifying them not at all.

● *The home situation*. Although a happy marriage does not guarantee safety, an unhappy one certainly doesn't help. "The pain of having a lack of intimacy and free flow of conversation in my marriage was too much for me to bear," one pastor wrote to me. "I longed to love with abandon, to feel feelings and share intimacies with someone else." He went on to describe a series of seven affairs over ten years.

Although such excessive needs for affection can be neurotic, the fact is that if a marriage is satisfying, a minister should be able to focus even his neurotic needs on his spouse. An affair easily can be encouraged when the need for intimacy is great and the marriage does not provide an opportunity for close sharing.

• *Life stages*. It is quite clear that men, in particular, are more vulnerable to affairs when they pass through critical stages of life. One of these is commonly called the midlife crisis, but there are other critical stages also. Almost every decade brings its own period of crisis, demanding a major adjustment of values and behavior.

Ministers do not escape these. If their work is not satisfying, or if they are having problems in the church, they are more prone to a crisis period. In times of burnout or interpersonal conflict, or when major life decisions must be made, the desire for comfort and emotional closeness increases dramatically.

Recognizing the Danger Signals

Since an intimate affair can develop almost unnoticed during counseling, a discussion of the danger signals is crucial.

1. One early signal of countertransference is when a pastor begins to look forward to the counseling sessions with a particular parishioner. He ruminates about the appointment and cannot wait for the time to arrive. His pulse rate increases, his palms become sweaty, and his voice develops a slight tremor when he sees her.

2. Very soon he begins to extend the session time and may even grant her extra counseling sessions. He cancels other appointments (often without even realizing he is doing it) to please her.

3. Hidden or oblique messages are sent both ways. The message, which on the surface is innocuous, means something more personal at a deeper level.

4. Counseling sessions may spend an inordinate amount of time on sexual matters. The parishioner may begin to share

sexual history or previous affairs that are quite unrelated to the problem for which counseling has been sought.

5. The pastor may begin to notice his own marital frustrations more. He begins to complain about petty things, often because he is feeling guilty and can alleviate this guilt by transforming it into anger.

6. He begins to fantasize excessively about his client. Sexual fantasies may focus on her exclusively.

7. He makes excuses to call her and have extra conversations with her. Luncheon appointments in a remote setting may then follow. These are rationalized as "additional counseling sessions."

8. Casual touching becomes more frequent, and the sessions end with embraces that become more prolonged or intense.

One particular personality type, the hysterical personality, is a very high risk for a minister to counsel. It has long been recognized in psychiatry that the difference between a brilliant psychiatrist and a less skilled one is that the first recognizes the hysterical personality and runs away faster. This should also be true for ministers!

The hysterical personality is typically shallow, overly reactive, even vivacious, uninhibited in displaying sexuality, given to flirtations, coquetry, and romantic fantasy. Such a person is also impressionable and craves excitement, but is naive and frigid. She is, in essence, a caricature of femininity, drawing attention to herself to obtain admiration.

Because this personality is extremely prone to transference, the pastor who falls prey to her seductions is bound to be destroyed. He may be embarrassed by public displays of affection and the discovery that her initial attractiveness was only superficial.

Dealing with Transference

The average pastor cannot afford the time and energy demanded by a counselee with a high propensity for transference. Training in dealing with transference problems requires extensive supervision, far more than is typically provided in a course on counseling. If this training is available, you should take advantage of it.

In the meantime:

• The safest way to deal with transference is simply to receive it as one would receive any feeling of a client. This is done without encouraging the transference any further. The counselor helps the client see that the feelings reside in her, not in the counselor.

The counselor may ask clarifying questions to increase the client's understanding of her feelings. "You feel you're in love with me. Why do you suppose this is so?" In other words, the full expression of feelings is allowed without either condoning or rejecting them.

• At a later stage, and only when it can be done without offending the client, the transference feelings are interpreted directly. For example, "Sometimes when people share their innermost secrets with someone else, they feel drawn and very close to that person. Do you think this is what is happening here?"

• Always stay professional. I don't mean you cannot be friendly and personable. I do mean that you keep to your appointment schedule and avoid stepping out of your professional role.

• Don't hesitate to make a referral to a trusted Christian psychotherapist if the transference gets out of hand. A mark of professional competence is knowing your limits.

The Pastor's Protection

But what about countertransference? What does a pastor do with those warm, loving feelings toward a parishioner?

• To begin with, never share these feelings with your counselee. Never talk of them or even hint that they are present. They are your problem, not your client's. If you do, you will either encourage the development of an intimate relationship, or you will be rejected. You lose both ways.

• Understand the difference between countertransference and simple attraction. In simple attraction, which is quite normal, you can walk away from the person to whom you feel some attraction. You are free to leave. You can choose to leave. But when you are obsessed with someone, allowing yourself to think about her constantly, you have problems. You must learn to redirect your thoughts and avoid fantasizing over the person to whom you feel attracted.

• Be aware of the power of your position, and pray that God will help you use it wisely. If you neurotically need excessive intimacy, praise, or admiration, get help for your problem.

• Develop a system of accountability. Not only are you accountable to God, but you need someone to share with honestly, a person to whom you can be accountable and talk frankly about your feelings. Such a person could be a work colleague, a pastor from another church (where the accountability can be reciprocated by yourself), or even your spouse.

The Pastor's Spouse

In fact, the spouse's role is extremely crucial in helping a pastor develop a safe position from which to counsel. Many wives find it difficult to understand how their husband, a pastor, can be attracted to another woman. How can a man so prominent, so respected, so intelligent, be subject to vulgar temptation?

As Paul Tournier points out in his book *To Understand Each Other*, this attitude only increases a pastor's guilt feelings and prevents him from sharing his innermost struggles over sex with her. To him, she becomes the incarnation of moral law. Tournier says, "This is the driving force of much adultery, so severely denounced by the virtuous . . . wife once she discovers it." She thinks that if he really loved her, he would not think of other women.

What she doesn't know is that her pastor/husband desperately wants to confide this struggle to her. He wants to channel his arousal back to her, where it belongs. But her veil of silence, resistance, and condemnation only increases the emotional distance.

From the viewpoint of Christian morality, this woman is right. But she has done nothing to help build a safer, more secure marriage from which her pastor/husband can minister to the fears, sufferings, sorrows, guilt, and misery of a lost world. The same is true from the woman's perspective when she encounters a husband who is not receptive to her feelings.

Tournier goes on to provide the soundest advice I have yet discovered on preventing illicit affairs in the ministry (or, for that matter, in any Christian marriage). He says, "The best protection against sexual temptations is to be able to speak honestly of them and to find, in the wife's understanding, without any trace of complicity whatsoever, effective and affective help needed to overcome them."

Coupled with a dependence upon God's Holy Spirit to provide help in time of trouble, this sort of transparency can prevent affairs. It can also build a depth of love, understanding, and oneness that I doubt can be experienced any other way this side of heaven.

SIX

AVOIDING THE SCARLET LETTER

A common path to sexual sin is the notion that feelings are not only all-important but also totally uncontrollable; they just happen to you.

LOUIS MCBURNEY

We're all shocked when we hear a respected fellow minister has been exposed as an adulterer. We think to ourselves, *Boy, what an idiot! I'll never do a thing like that,* and we mean every word of it. We're as convinced of it as any commitment we've ever made.

Almost every minister I've counseled who found himself entangled in sexual infidelity had that same confidence. I can remember only two men who consciously set out for sexual conquest. One seriously questioned his masculinity and sought to prove himself through repeated sexual encounters. The other was sociopathic and used others impulsively for his own pleasure or profit in many ways, including sexually.

What derailed all the others, who were so sure it could never happen to them? Although they were neither deeply disturbed in their sexual identity nor sociopathic, they did neglect some important principles and crucial warning signs. By becoming more aware of these, we can avoid falling into an adulterous affair and earning our scarlet letter.

Recognizing Our Vulnerability

Men in ministry are especially vulnerable to sexual temptation because they work in what is often a female subculture, the church. Simply their presence on the job exposes them to potential romantic or sexual relationships.

In addition, our world is rapidly removing the restraints to sexual involvement. Men and women are even encouraged to "find themselves" through sexual encounters. Perhaps some women in your church flirt with that very idea. Or with you.

Another reason for increased vulnerability is the similarity between spirituality and sexuality. In both, we lower personal barriers, encourage intimacy, become open and vulnerable, and experience profoundly moving emotions. Some individuals compare their deepest spiritual moments to sexual climax. Both provide an intense response, a loss of ego boundaries, a sense of oneness with those who share the experience.

Our personality also makes us more vulnerable. As sensitive, caring, giving persons, we resemble a warm living room for the lonely and dependent. Thousands of people, single and married alike, seek closeness. Most married women name as their primary marital problem their husband's insensitivity to their emotional needs. It makes them desperate for a companion who will talk with them and listen.

Enter the minister, the model husband. As long as they don't consult our wives, women may see us as ideal — strong and capable, yet gentle, warm, and loving. The church even encourages us to be that sensitive person to everyone in need, which includes many lonely women, whose activity in the church masks hunger for attention and affection. Both our personal warmth and our professional calling put us in jeopardy.

From my experience, I'd identify yet another danger — the angry seductress. Some women cherish a deep, inner hatred for men and a compulsion to gain control over them. Frequently they were rejected or abused by their fathers. Often they learned in childhood and adolescence that sensuality is their most effective weapon. Consciously or unconsciously, they form a pattern of conquests while they appear to be helpless women who need a strong man to care for them.

What man of the cloth is not eager to help damsels in distress? Yet many pastors who have ridden to the rescue find themselves seduced, exposed, and expelled in short order. The "helpless damsel" sometimes even garners the love and compassion of the church. She plots her next assault while the unsuspecting minister is still trying to remove the tar and feathers. One such woman had been the hapless "victim" of sexual advances by the last three pastors in her church. All had left in disgrace, their ministries nullified.

A minister is a particularly enticing target for this kind of woman. With a man of God, she can act out her hostility toward men in general, authority figures, symbolic fathers of society, and even God the Father all at once. It gives a gratifying sense of power. She again proves the male to be weak and inadequate.

It's also critical that we know our own particular vulnerability. Only I am aware of my individual sexual thoughts and drives. I may have frustrations with marital sex or doubts about my potency. I may find certain female physical characteristics particularly tempting. Midlife transition may raise questions about what I've been missing or how long I can continue to function successfully. Any of these issues may contribute to my vulnerability to an affair.

Maintaining Our Safety

Given our vocational vulnerability, how do we protect ourselves?

Primarily (if we are married), we must maintain our marriages — have a continuous romantic affair with our first love, put some of our creativity into rekindling those fires of passion. Most of those who get into trouble have allowed marriage to become dull, unsatisfying, even unfriendly.

Tell the truth: Do you look forward to being home with your wife? Does she make you feel you're the most wonderful man in the world? Do you light up her life in a special way? Does she light up yours? Do you find yourself distracted from work at times by fantasies of your lover at home? Maybe we need to court our best girlfriend.

Without a doubt, being in love with our mates provides the

best defense against a sexual affair. If we're not there now, it may take months of inventive, energetic courting to relight that fire, but it can be done as we build on the foundation of our commitment — not on our present feelings.

The second defense: reassessing our attitudes about falling in love. A common path to sexual sin is the notion that feelings are not only all-important but also totally uncontrollable; they just happen to you. A story I hear frequently from the adulterous minister is "I had no intention of becoming involved with her, but suddenly we realized we were deeply in love." He makes it appear he was strolling along innocently one sunny day and was suddenly caught in a thunderstorm. Once it struck, he was soaked to the skin and powerless to dry himself. In fact, it felt so good he didn't *want* to dry off. He was glad he'd forgotten his umbrella.

Now, I confess, I like women. I find females exciting, fun, intriguing, nice to the senses, and often more comfortable companions than men. I suspect many of you could make the same confession. Feeling as I do, I could conceivably fall in love with a different woman every other day if I allowed my feelings free rein. But I don't. I keep a tight rein on my feelings.

One further caution: A commonly held notion claims you can be genuinely in love with two people simultaneously. That rationalization tries to give me permission to fall in love with another woman without admitting unfaithfulness to my wife. Don't believe it! Jesus' words about your heart being where your treasure is apply to romantic relationships as well as the kingdom. When we begin to invest emotional energy, we store up treasure in the object of our attention. Our hearts will follow. Treasure cannot be invested equally in two people. We must not kid ourselves. We do have control over where we put our treasure. When we find ourselves contemplating doing that special something for the other woman, we must redirect that energy into our marriage relationship.

A third defense: Avoid every appearance of evil, and every

opportunity. I've learned to exercise care about being alone with a woman. Long periods alone not only raise suspicion but can leave us vulnerable to false accusations or intense temptation. Every time my college roommate went out on a date, he would ask me to pray that he'd "have temptation to withstand." Naturally he sought only to "develop his spiritual strength!" That's not a recommended technique for building ministerial defenses.

One pastor told me an attractive young woman began attending his church. She was a new Christian, but he soon discovered her sordid history. She had many problems and started asking his advice. Then she requested counseling. Because of her job, she could come only in the evening after the church secretary was gone. At first he said no, but she was so persistent, in such need, and seemed so sweet, he finally gave in. Dropping his guard proved his undoing.

Alone with him in his office, she closed the door and pulled the curtains. Before he knew what was happening, she was sitting on his lap, unbuttoning her blouse, exposing her braless breasts. She threw her arms around his neck and confessed her burning desire for him.

Now, while you fantasize about that situation, let me tell you quickly that what followed was no dream. It was a nightmare. He did succumb, but he declared they couldn't let it happen again. She threatened to tell all if he didn't continue to see her. Then she began to tell all anyway — to his wife, to other church members, and finally to one of the elders. The church board ultimately confronted him and asked him to resign. His wife almost left him, but fortunately she recognized the pathology of the seductive woman and forgave her foolish husband. They had a lot of rebuilding to do, and his guilt nearly destroyed him.

We simply must avoid all appearance of evil. No matter how safe and innocent the situation may seem, it can sour in the twinkling of an eye or the popping of a button.

Blatant seduction, however, is unusual. More often we

need to guard against a far more subtle pattern. The most common story of infidelity involves an attractive, committed church member who seeks counsel for marital problems. She is neither seductive nor sociopathic, but rather a thoughtful, wholesome, sensitive woman whom the minister had not particularly noticed as a stunning beauty. She is lonely and neglected by her husband, who doesn't communicate. The pastor does listen, and she appreciates him for it. She begins to show her gratitude in many ways, particularly with her praise. That feels good, and the pastor begins to enjoy the attention and affirmation. He gradually realizes what a truly insightful person she is.

This is the critical crossroads in the relationship: it can remain professional or slide into a romantic affair. It's a point of decision. We either set limits on time with her, guard against her romantic fantasies (and our own), work on involving her husband in counseling (perhaps referring them both to another professional), and avoid comparing her with our wives; or we may make a costly mistake.

A decidedly dangerous, yet completely conscious behavior often begins at this point. It may seem justified as an innocent, even helpful, thing to do. We might convince ourselves we are only identifying with our client and modeling openness, but it is a fatal choice. That drastic mistake is to share with her our own inner hurts and the areas of our marital disappointment. I know of no other single event that so dramatically shifts the direction of a relationship. Then I am no longer a helpful, concerned counselor; I have become a lonely man who needs her love. It's as destructive and decisive as reaching for a zipper.

All the barriers come down, and counselor and client begin to focus on each other's needs. Intense energy flows into the relationship. The two feel they were meant for each other — this love is so perfect it must be ordained by God (a frequent rationalization). Such feelings become so overwhelming that sexual involvement is a natural by-product. What began as an innocent professional relationship burns out of control. They are possessed.

External Danger Signs

Anywhere along this flower-strewn path to destruction we can back off and escape if we recognize the danger and understand the disastrous consequences. A quarterback approaching the line of scrimmage assesses the defensive alignment. When he senses a blitz, he may change the play to protect himself from being sacked. We also need to recognize the warning signs that indicate a blitz of the heart, and quickly call an audible. Here are a few of the indications I watch for in the other woman.

● *Growing dependence.* She may express this in many ways. The most common is increasing requests for my time. Ostensibly legitimate crises arise that demand my attention. She may also want me to make decisions for her or to give my approval for what she does.

● *Affirmation and praise.* We're all vulnerable to being complimented. It feels especially good if we're not getting much praise at home. One pastor told me his difficult choice to either go home to criticism or be with the other woman who understood and admired him.

● *Complaints about loneliness.* She may begin to confess that her loneliness seems even worse now that she knows what meaningful companionship is like. Now she escapes the hurt and pain with me. I am the only one who has ever done that for her. What a hook!

● *Giving gifts.* No matter how trivial the gifts may seem, they can be a serious indication of her increasing emotional investment. She is thinking about me and how to make me happy. A sense of obligation on my part may soon develop.

● *Physical contact.* This usually begins in innocent ways — brief nudging of bodies in a crowded room or a light touch of her hand on the arm — but it can escalate to a hug of gratitude or a "holy kiss" that communicates more than sisterly affection. A common occurrence is a woman saying, "You've helped me so much, Pastor. Can I just give you a hug to show my appreciation?"

This doesn't apply to physical contact with every female in my life. Many innocent hugs show warmth and caring on a purely platonic level. You know the difference as well as I. I'm very careful about touching some women, either because of signals from them or feelings of attraction within myself. Yet there are many others whom I can embrace quite safely.

● *Other seductive behavior.* I notice how a woman dresses, whether she wears perfume, makes subtle suggestions or jokes about my irresistibility as a man, sends messages about her availability when her husband is away, or increasingly talks about sexuality in the counseling sessions. She may begin to report dreams about us together in romantic situations.

I have learned to spot these red flags for my own safety.

Internal Dangers Signs

These same signs, as well as others, may also lurk within me. Using the quarterback illustration, it's as though I realize my running backs occupy the wrong position for the play I've called. I may need to call time-out to get the team rearranged so I don't make a costly mistake.

Here are some inner signals I monitor:

● *Thinking about her.* At first I may explain this as my professional interest in her problems, but the focus slowly shifts from her problems to her person. This is not necessarily sexual. More likely it involves her personality traits and behavior patterns. Pleasant feelings build around the positive new relationship. It's only natural to enjoy them and begin to reflect on the experience.

● *Comparing her to my wife.* The other woman always looks better than a wife. She is new, different, and usually seen at her best. She is well groomed, exudes positive vibes, and isn't demanding. She laughs at my jokes; she thinks I'm fascinating. Suddenly a wife's faults begin to look bigger. I eventually tell my wife she should be more like Mrs. Jones in some way or another.

• *Finding excuses to be with her.* This will probably be in group situations at first. Usually many opportunities occur to see her in the church context. It's amazing what a truly significant part of the ministry the youth fellowship clean-up committee can suddenly become.

• *Beginning to have sexual fantasies about her.* These may occur while working in the office or while looking at her during a worship service. They are likely to progress to masturbatory images or even intrude upon marital lovemaking.

• *Scheming ways to be alone.* Arranging to be at group events is one thing, but inventing ways to be alone is quite another. Invariably this calls for some degree of deception. It starts by lying to one's wife and secretary. The lying multiplies, and manufacturing alibis becomes frequent. There follows an increasing irritability toward your wife's demands for attention or her expressions of suspicion. Isn't it interesting that I could resent my wife's legitimate claim to my affection? It is as though she has become an intruder into my private life.

Wives are, in fact, one of our most important protective screens. They are often much more sensitive to other females threatening their territory. We may be oblivious to some of the early nonverbal signs, or they may just be flattering enough that we don't want them to stop. If we learn to listen to our wives, they may save us from becoming too involved in a potentially destructive relationship.

• *Wanting to share my marital problems with the client.* "My wife hasn't been sensitive to my needs, either. She isn't a good partner sexually. She doesn't understand me as a person or show me the respect I deserve." The more I complain about my mate, the more unhappy I will feel about my marriage, and the more appealing the other woman appears. To complicate matters, that other woman probably does care about me and must struggle to keep her nurturing instincts separated from her romantic attraction. It is a losing situation.

Settle for an "F"

The problem of adultery is as difficult as the dangers are real. Why else would so many seriously committed ministers fall into it? The vulnerability of our position on the one hand and the powerful effect of feelings on the other set us up.

Only by staying alert to the possibility of trouble, keeping our marriage vital and growing, and watching for the danger signs can we be sure to survive. We can do it. We do have a choice.

For once in our lives, let's not strive for an "A" — at least not the scarlet variety. Let's settle for a true-blue "F" — for faithful.

SEVEN

STRATEGIES TO KEEP FROM FALLING

I now live with the frightening but powerfully motivating knowledge that I could commit sexual immorality. I started taking precautions to keep it from happening to me.

RANDY C. ALCORN

Something terrible has happened." The tense voice was my friend's, calling from across the country. "Yesterday our pastor left his wife and ran off with another woman."

I was sad, but not shocked or even surprised. Fifteen years ago I would have been shocked. Ten years ago I would have been surprised. But I've heard the same story too many times now ever to be surprised again.

I recently spoke on sexual purity at a Bible college. During that week, many students came for counseling, including three I'll call Rachel, Barb, and Pam.

Rachel got right to the point: "My parents sent me to one of our pastors for counseling, and I ended up sleeping with him." Later the same day, Barb, a church leader's daughter, told me through tears, "My dad has had sex with me for years, and now he's starting on my sisters." The next evening I met with Pam. Her story? "I came to Bible college to get away from an affair with my pastor."

For every well-known Christian television personality or author whose impropriety is widely publicized, there are any number of lesser-known pastors, Bible teachers, and parachurch workers who quietly resign or are fired for sexual immorality. Most of us can name several. The myth that ministers are morally invulnerable dies slowly, however, even in the face of overwhelming evidence. But there never has been a mystical antibody that makes us immune to sexual sin. Even those of us who haven't fallen know how fierce is the struggle with temptation.

Furthermore, ministry brings with it serious built-in hazards, moral land mines that can destroy us, our families, and our churches. Among them: our position of influence and that strange blend of ego-feeding flattery and debilitating criticism, which can fill us with either pride or despair. As a result, our perspective can be warped, our resistance to temptation diminished. In addition, our endless tasks and the consequent disorienting fatigue can make us oblivious to what's really happening to us.

I recall with embarrassment my naiveté as a young pastor. Every time I heard the stories of Christian leaders falling into sexual sin, I thought, *It could never happen to me.*

What level of pride is required to believe that sexual sin could overtake Samson, David ("a man after God's own heart"), Solomon, and a host of modern Christian leaders, but not *me?* Paul's warning in 1 Corinthians 10 deserves a prominent place on our dashboards, desks, or Day-Timers: "If you think you are standing firm, be careful that you don't fall."

Fortunately, I wised up. The person who believes he will never be burglarized leaves his doors and windows open, and cash on the top of his dresser. Likewise, the one who thinks the danger isn't real invariably takes risks that wind up proving costly. I now live with the frightening but powerfully motivating knowledge that I *could* commit sexual immorality. I started taking precautions to keep it from happening to me.

Practical Guidelines for Sexual Purity

Monitoring my spiritual pulse. Often those who fall into sexual sin can point back to lapses in their practices of meditation, worship, prayer, and the healthy self-examination such disciplines foster. All of us know this, but in the busyness of giving out, we easily can neglect the replenishing of our spiritual reservoirs.

Daily disciplines are important, of course, but I've found that for me they're not enough. God gave Israel not merely one hour a day but one day a week, several weeks a year, and even one year every seven to break the pattern of life long enough to worship and reflect and take stock.

I periodically take overnight retreats by myself or with my wife. In times of greater need I've been away a week, usually in a cabin on the Oregon coast. This is not a vacation but a time in which the lack of immediate demands and the absence of noise give clarity to the still, small voice of God that is too easily drowned in the busyness of my daily life.

Guarding my marriage. I find I must regularly evaluate my relationship with my wife. In particular, I watch for the red flags of discontentment, poor communication, and poor sexual relationship. We try to spend regular, uninterrupted time together to renew our spiritual, intellectual, emotional, and physical closeness.

Many Christian leaders move so freely and deeply in the world of great spiritual truths and activities that unless they take pains to communicate daily, their spouses get left out. This development of two separate worlds leads to two separate lives and is often the first step toward an adulterous affair with "someone who understands me and my world."

Communication is key because every adultery begins with a deception, and most deceptions begin with seemingly innocent secrets, things "she doesn't need to know."

At work, I surround myself with reminders of my spouse and children — pictures, drawings, and mementos. When traveling, I make contact with my wife as often as possible. If I'm struggling with temptation, I try to be honest and ask for prayer. Fierce loyalty to our wives is also a key; I try always to speak highly of my wife in public and never to downgrade her to others. And I'm careful not to discuss my marriage problems with anyone of the opposite sex.

Further, my wife and I avail ourselves of many of the good books, tapes, and seminars geared to improving marriage. When my wife and I went on a Marriage Encounter weekend, we were surprised to discover some differences in perspective that, if left unaddressed, could have caused problems down the road.

Taking precautions. One pastor found his thoughts were continually drawn to a co-worker, more so than to his own wife. After months of rationalizing, he finally admitted to himself that he was looking for reasons to spend time with her. Then his rule of thumb became: I will meet with her only when necessary, only as long as necessary, only at the office, and with others present as much as possible. In time, his relationship with her returned to its original, healthy, co-worker status.

The questions with which I check myself: *Do I look forward in a special way to my appointments with this person? Would I rather see her than my wife? Do I seek to meet with her away from my office in a more casual environment? Do I prefer that my co-workers not know I'm meeting with her again?* An affirmative answer to any of these questions is, for me, a warning light.

Dealing with the subtle signs of sexual attraction. There's a mystique about spiritual ministry that some women find attractive. Their attitude toward the pastor can border on infatuation. It's flattering for the pastor, who perhaps is nursing fresh wounds from the last board meeting, to receive attention from an attractive woman who obviously admires him and hangs on his every word. (The deacons *jumped* on his every word.) Often the woman's husband is spiritually dead or weak. Finding him unworthy of her respect, she transfers her affection to this wonderfully spiritual man, her pastor. This is usually unconscious and therefore all the more dangerous.

She may send notes of appreciation or small gifts; he may reciprocate. Expressions of affection may inch beyond the healthy brother/sister variety. The hands are held tightly in prayer; the arm lingers a bit longer on the shoulder; the embraces become frequent.

All this seems harmless enough, but a subtle, powerful process of soul merger can occur. If things are not good on the home front, the pastor will, consciously or unconsciously, compare this woman to his wife, who may be noticeably *un*appreciative and *un*infatuated with him. This comparison is deadly and, unless it's stopped, can lead into covert romantic affection, which often leads to adultery.

A relationship can be sexual long before it becomes erotic. Just because I'm not touching a woman, or just because I'm not envisioning specific erotic encounters, does not mean I'm not becoming sexually involved with her. The erotic is usually not the beginning but the culmination of sexual attraction. Most pastors who end up in bed with a woman do it not just to gratify a sexual urge, but because they believe they've begun really to love her.

I once casually asked a woman about her obvious interest in a married man with whom she worked. "We're just friends," she responded with a defensiveness that indicated they weren't. "It's purely platonic, nothing sexual at all." In a matter of months, however, the two friends found themselves sneaking off from their families to be with each other, and finally their "friendship" developed into an affair that destroyed both of their marriages.

Lust isn't just unbridled passion. Even when it's "bridled" it may lead us down a path that our conscience could not have condoned had we experienced it in a more obvious, wanton way. Thus, our enemies are not only lascivious thoughts of sex but "innocuous" feelings of infatuation as well.

Backing off early. When meeting a woman for our third counseling appointment, I became aware that she was interested in me personally. What was more frightening was that I realized I subconsciously had sensed this before but had enjoyed her attraction too much to address the problem. Though I wasn't *yet* emotionally involved or giving her inappropriate attention, I wasn't deflecting hers toward me, either, and was thereby inviting it.

I felt tempted to dismiss the matter as unimportant, "knowing" I would never get involved with her. Fortunately, when God prompted me, I knew I was no longer the right person to meet with her. I made other counseling arrangements for her.

Clearing cloudy thoughts. Often we justify our flirtations with logical, even spiritual, rationalizations. One pastor didn't tell his wife about his frequent meetings with a particular woman on the grounds he shouldn't violate confidentialities, even to his wife. Besides, he sensed his wife would be jealous (without good reason, of course), so why upset her? Under the cloak of professionalism and sensitivity to his wife, he proceeded to meet with this woman secretly. The result was predictable.

Another pastor had been struggling with lustful thoughts toward a college girl in his church. Rather than dealing with his struggles alone with the Lord, with a mature brother, or with his wife, he took the girl out to lunch to talk with *her*. Citing the biblical mandate to confess our sins and make things right with the person we've wronged, he told her, "I've been having lustful thoughts about you, and I felt I needed to confess them to you." Embarrassed but flattered, the girl began to entertain her own thoughts toward him, and finally they became sexually involved.

All this came from what the pastor told himself was a spiritual and obedient decision to meet with the girl. To misuse Scripture in this way and violate rules of wisdom and common sense shows how cloudy and undependable our thinking can become.

Holding myself accountable. Perhaps nowhere is more said and less done than in the area of accountability. From talking with Christian leaders, I've come to understand that the more prominent they become, the more they need accountability and the less they get it. As a church grows, often the pastors come to know many people but on a shallower level, and those around them think, *Who am I to ask him if this is a wise choice he's making?*

Many pastors in small churches also feel isolated, and even those in large churches with multiple staff members are usually Lone Rangers (without a Tonto) when it comes to facing their moral struggles. In a church with several pastors, one tried to discuss "something personal" three weeks in a row at staff meeting, but each time he was preempted because of a busy agenda. The fourth week his fellow pastors listened — three days *after* he had committed adultery.

Seven full-timers and several part-timers share pastoral responsibilities at our church. For several years now we have committed the first two hours of our weekly all-day staff meeting to discussing personal "sufferings and rejoicings" (1 Cor. 12:26), telling each other the state of our spiritual lives, and seeking and offering prayer and advice. We make sure no one is left out. We ask "How are you doing?" and if the answers are vague or something seems wrong, we probe deeper.

At first, this felt risky. It involved entrusting our reputations to others and opening ourselves to their honest investigation. But what actually results is usually positive encouragement. The risks, we found, are small compared to the rewards. Unlike many pastors, we don't feel alone in the ministry. We know each other's imperfections, and we have nothing to prove to each other. These hours of weekly accountability have become weekly therapy, and no matter how full the agenda, we are committed to keeping in touch with each other's inner lives.

Pastors without other staff can find a lay person or two or a nearby pastor who will love them as they are *and* regularly ask the questions of accountability. What questions are those? Usually the questions we least want to answer. And Howard Hendricks suggests that after all the hard questions are asked, the final question should be, "In your answers to any of the previous questions, did you lie?"

This kind of accountability can produce amazing results.

Once I was undergoing a time of strong sexual temptation, and finally I called a friend with whom I was having breakfast the next day. I said, "Please pray for me, and ask me tomorrow morning what I did." He agreed, and the moment I put down the phone the temptation was gone. Why? I'd like to say it was because I'm so spiritual, but the truth is there was no way I was going to face my friend the next morning and have to tell him I had sinned.

Guarding my mind. A battering ram may hit a fortress gate a thousand times, and no one time seems to have an effect, yet finally the gate caves in. Likewise, immorality is the cumulative product of small mental indulgences and minuscule compromises, the immediate consequences of which were, at the time, indiscernible.

Our thoughts are the fabric with which we weave our character and destiny. No, we can't avoid all sexual stimuli, but in Martin Luther's terms, "You can't keep the birds from flying over your head, but you can keep them from making a nest in your hair."

I like to put it another way: "If you're on a diet, don't go into a doughnut shop." For me this means such practical things as staying away from the magazine racks, video stores, advertisements, programs, images, people, and places that tempt me to lust.

One man who travels extensively told me about a practice that has helped to guard his mind from immorality. "Whenever I check into my hotel," he said, "where I normally stay for three or four days, I ask them at the front desk to please remove the television from my room. Invariably they look at me like I'm crazy, and then they say, 'But sir, if you don't want to watch it, you don't have to turn it on.' Since I'm a paying customer, however, I politely insist, and I've never once been refused.

"The point is, I know that in my weak and lonely moments late in the evening, I'll be tempted to watch the immoral movies that are only one push of a button away. In the past I've succumbed to that temptation over and over, but not anymore. Having the television removed in my stronger moments has been my way of saying, 'I'm serious about this, Lord,' and it's been the key to victory in my battle against impurity."

Regularly rehearsing the consequences. I met with a man who had been a leader in a Christian organization until he fell into immorality. I asked him, "What could have been done to prevent this?"

He paused for only a moment, then said with haunting pain and precision, "If only I had really known, really thought through, what it would cost me and my family and my Lord, I honestly believe I never would have done it."

In the wake of several Christian leaders' falling into immorality, a co-pastor and I developed a list of specific consequences that would result from our immorality. The list was devastating, and to us it spoke more powerfully than any sermon or article on the subject. *(See end of chapter.)*

Periodically, especially when traveling or in a time of weakness, we read through the list. In a tangible and personal way, it brings home God's inviolate law of choice and consequence, cutting through the fog of rationalization and filling our hearts with the healthy, motivating fear of God.

Winning the Battle

In J. R. R. Tolkien's book *The Hobbit*, there was no one seemingly more invincible than Smaug, the mighty dragon. But then that unlikely hero, Bilbo Baggins, found one small weak spot in Smaug's underbelly. That information, in the hands of a skilled marksman, was all it took to seal the doom of the presumptuous dragon. Unaware of his weakness and underestimating his opponents, Smaug failed to protect himself. An arrow pierced his heart, and the dragon was felled.

An exciting story with a happy ending. But when it's a Christian leader felled, the ending is not so happy. It's tragic. The Evil One knows only too well the weak spots of the most mighty Christian warriors, not to mention the rest of us. He isn't one to waste his arrows, bouncing them harmlessly off the strongest plates of our spiritual armor. His aim is deadly, and it is at our points of greatest vulnerability that he will most certainly attack.

We are in battle — a battle far more fierce and strategic than any Alexander, Hannibal, or Napoleon ever fought. We must realize that no one prepares for a battle of which he is unaware, and no ones wins a battle for which he doesn't prepare.

As we more and more hear of Christian leaders succumbing to immorality, we must not say merely, "There, but for the grace of God, I might have gone," rather, "There, but for the grace of God — and but for my alertness and diligence in the spiritual battle — I may *yet* go."

Consequences of a Moral Tumble

Whenever I feel particularly vulnerable to sexual temptation, I find it helpful to review what effects my action could have:

- Grieving the Lord who redeemed me.
- Dragging his sacred name into the mud.
- One day having to look Jesus, the Righteous Judge, in the face and give an account of my actions.
- Following in the footsteps of these people whose immorality forfeited their ministries and caused me to shudder: (list names)
- Inflicting untold hurt on Nanci, my best friend and loyal wife.
- Losing Nanci's respect and trust.
- Hurting my beloved daughters, Karina and Angie.
- Destroying my example and credibility with my children, and nullifying both present and future efforts to teach them to obey God ("Why listen to a man who betrayed Mom and us?").
- If my blindness should continue or my wife be unable to forgive, perhaps losing my wife and my children forever.

- Causing shame to my family ("Why isn't Daddy a pastor anymore?").
- Losing self-respect.
- Creating a form of guilt awfully hard to shake. Even though God would forgive me, would I forgive myself?
- Forming memories and flashbacks that could plague future intimacy with my wife.
- Wasting years of ministry training and experience for a long time, maybe permanently.
- Forfeiting the effect of years of witnessing to my father and reinforcing his distrust for ministers that has only begun to soften by my example but that would harden, perhaps permanently, because of my immorality.
- Undermining the faithful example and hard work of other Christians in our community.
- Bringing great pleasure to Satan, the enemy of God and all that is good.
- Heaping judgment and endless difficulty on the person with whom I committed adultery.
- Possibly bearing the physical consequences of such diseases as gonorrhea, syphilis, chlamydia, herpes, and AIDS; perhaps infecting Nanci or, in the case of AIDS, even causing her death.
- Possibly causing pregnancy, with the personal and financial implications, including a lifelong reminder of my sin.
- Bringing shame and hurt to these fellow pastors and elders: (list names)
- Causing shame and hurt to these friends, especially those I've led to Christ and discipled: (list names)
- Invoking shame and life-long embarrassment upon myself.

PART III
PASTORAL RESPONSES

Counseling rule number one: if possible, get counselees out of the environment that is causing their problem. Remove alcoholics from bars, keep drug addicts out of opium dens, and tell overeaters to lock the refrigerator.

Unfortunately, pastors don't have that luxury. Sexual temptation is impossible to avoid altogether. It pervades our culture. Consider these factors:

— Pornography became the focus of national attention with the Attorney General's Commission and its landmark 1987 report, which among other things, documented the rapid spread of porn in recent years. "Sales have never been better in the pornography trade," reported U.S. News & World Report of the $8 billion annual business.

— The VCR, barely known five years ago, has made sexually oriented material much more easily available and brought it into many homes for the first time. Sales of hard-core porn videos, for example, more than doubled from 1983 to 1986.

— This trend has not spared church members. According to our survey of Christianity Today magazine lay people, 45 percent indicate they have done something they consider sexually inappropriate. Twenty-three percent admit they have had extramarital intercourse.

Church leaders must help these people. But help in a way that doesn't put themselves in compromising positions.

There are several ways to do this.

One is to learn specific counseling techniques to use for different sexual problems. Several of the chapters in this section deal with these specific problems:

Gary Sweeten and Hal Schell, who minister at College Hill Presbyterian Church in Cincinnati, Ohio, write in Chapter 8 about "Counseling Sexual Addicts," how to deal with people who have all the earmarks of being addicted to sex. Sexual addiction is a category increasingly recognized by psychologists as having similar dynamics to drug or alcohol addiction.

Danny Armstrong, a military chaplain, gives advice on how to handle a special class of sexually abused counselees in Chapter 9, "Counseling Rape Victims."

Others are abused as children. Michael Phillips, pastor of Lake Windermere Alliance Church, Invermere, British Columbia, tells how these young experiences can have devastating results—and what you can do to help. See Chapter 10, "Counseling Victims of Sexual Abuse."

A second way to guard yourself while helping others is to understand the interpersonal dynamics that go into relationships with certain counselees. Andre Bustanoby, a marriage and family therapist in suburban Washington, D.C., gives solid counsel on what to expect in Chapter 11, "Counseling the Seductive Female."

A third way is to apply loving discipline. A side benefit of holding others to God's sexual standards is that you renew your own commitment to those standards. Sometimes discipline takes the form of firmly applying scriptural truths about sexual matters to those sitting in your office. Gregory Stover gives sound advice on how to dispense truth to unmarried couples who have jumped the gun on sexual matters. Chapter 12, "Lovingly Leveling With Live-Ins," represents wisdom from his ministry as pastor of Church of the Cross United Methodist, Toledo, Ohio.

EIGHT

COUNSELING THE SEXUALLY ADDICTED

Resisting temptation really means resisting the feelings of condemnation that cause a person to seek sexual relief.

HAL B. SCHELL AND
GARY SWEETEN

We'd like you to meet some of our friends.

Don is a rising young attorney whose future holds great potential. He has a beautiful wife, Toni, three lovely children, a large home, and important social standing in the church and community. Yet despite these outward signs of success and a solid emotional and sexual relationship with Toni, two or three times a week Don compulsively visits prostitutes and porno shops.

Claire is a high-priced call girl. Like most prostitutes, Claire hates sex. But desperate for male affection, she attempts time after time to prove her self-worth by selling "love" to any man who will pay the price.

Jan is a 35-year-old church musician who grew up in a pious, Bible-based home. He attended a small Christian college and went on to seminary. Married with two children, Jan has been involved in homosexual activities since a professor seduced him in college. He came to us after being picked up for sexual imposition in the restroom of a department store.

These three are composites of people who have come to Spring Forth, College Hill Presbyterian Church's ministry for sexual addicts. As you can see, sexual addicts aren't always the dregs of society. Often they're men and women highly successful in their fields, yet they involve themselves compulsively in sexual activities through which they are bound to be caught and humiliated.

To show some of the dynamics of counseling the sexual addict, we've developed a scenario for our ministry to Jan.

Establish Trust

Jan called because he'd been arrested. The initial phone call came to Hal, director of our Spring Forth ministry. Hal listened carefully and compassionately to Jan's crisis and agreed to meet with him for more discussion the next night at 7:30. Hal told Jan the session would include another counselor because we always minister in teams of two persons who are usually the same sex as the counselee.

Before the appointment, Hal and Gary spent time in prayer. We wanted to be sure not to show repugnance toward Jan, even though we viewed his behavior as wrong. We asked God to enable us to model his grace, love, and acceptance. Friends of the same sex who relate in caring but nonerotic ways are crucial in the healing of sexual addicts.

Jan, at the first session, blasted the police for their lack of concern about "real criminals." We listened to his strong feelings and irrational thoughts, knowing they covered deeper feelings of guilt and shame.

Our initial goal is to establish trust and openness. We want to show the love Jesus showed to the woman caught in adultery. So, although we didn't agree with Jan's condemnation of the police, neither did we confront his blame-shifting behavior. After about forty-five minutes, we attempted to get Jan to look more carefully at himself: "Jan, how does this make you feel about yourself?" When Jan saw he was not being condemned, he began to show his true feelings of guilt and condemnation. Again, we listened respectfully as Jan turned his full wrath onto himself.

The volcano of emotions that had been directed at others just minutes before now came full force back to himself. Although the battle was far from over, we at least had gotten to the place of focusing on a real enemy.

Jan knew he was the problem but didn't know how to change. As Jeremiah 17:9 states, "The heart is deceitful and corrupt, and no one understands it." Jan was confused about the causes of his behavior. Like Paul, he knew in his mind what was right but found another law in his flesh that kept him from doing what was right.

Our closing prayer in that first session emphasized two points: First, that God would speak love and grace to his son Jan. Second, that the Holy Spirit would reveal the broken pieces of Jan's heart to him in preparation for our next meeting. In addition, we made a covenant to pray for Jan daily for protection and strength.

After Jan left, we decided to spend the next few sessions getting a personal and family history, looking for patterns of rejection, emotional trauma, and sexual dysfunction. We also wanted to see what role Jan was assigned in his family as he grew up.

Discover Patterns

Early in the second interview, we uncovered a powerful pattern in Jan's family. There was a long history of fathers who were absent through alcohol, divorce, or work, and the predictable pattern of overly concerned mothers whose presence smothered the children.

Jan was the fourth of six children, with three older brothers. By the time of Jan's conception, the entire family desperately wanted a girl. Jan's maternal grandmother chose the unborn baby's name — Janet — after her mother, the saintly matriarch of the family. The closets were filled with frilly, pink dresses, and everyone excitedly waited for little Janet to be born.

When Jan was born, though they did change the name to

make it appropriate for a boy, Mother reinforced the rejection by dressing him like a little girl and introducing him as her little boy-girl. Jan actually learned to live as a female and played the role of a girl in the home.

The more Mother babied Jan and enmeshed him into her own emotional system, the more Father withdrew. He was proud only of sons who were good at hard labor and athletics. He disliked Jan and his "sissy music." Although Jan excelled as a singer, arranger, and pianist, he developed a negative self-image, even to the point of saying he hated himself for being trapped in a man's body.

We also discovered the relationship with his older brothers and younger sister was no better than that with his father. The older brothers continually put Jan down. For example, the oldest brother had a favorite TV chair he guarded jealously. If Jan sat in the chair, Steve would lift him out of it and throw him down on the floor, a gesture that literally, as well as symbolically, "put Jan in his place."

By age 6, Jan "knew" he was different from other boys; they were more masculine than he. These beliefs led to feelings of discomfort in the presence of males, and as a result, he ate in order to gain a lot of weight to give himself protection from other boys. However, that led to classmates' jokes and the nickname "Butterball," all of which reinforced the rejection and shame he already perceived and kept Jan from developing friendships with other males.

A particularly devastating experience occurred when Jan was about 13. Being in the nude together in the swimming hole was not unusual for the entire family. On one occasion, a younger sister pointed at Jan's genitals and giggled, "Your thing is so small you'll never be a man."

Sexual addiction is usually the result of perceived trauma, neglect, or rejection at an early age. Such trauma often results in symbolic confusion between sexuality and sexual identity. Although the sexuality (biological gender) of a child is known at birth, sexual identity (masculinity or femininity) is learned from parents — especially the father. In fact, we consider this one of the father's principal roles, because when he doesn't affirm his children's sexual identity, great spiritual, emotional, and sexual damage can result.

Jan's lack of fatherly affirmation caused him to believe he was not good; anybody who really knew him wouldn't love or accept him. Jan was convinced he could trust nobody to meet his true needs, not even God.

Because a homosexual's belief system often causes friendship and warmth to be perceived in erotic ways, we were prepared when Jan made his pass toward Gary just prior to our third meeting. Arriving early, he not-so-subtly asked Gary for a date.

Years before, the first time a counselee had done this, Gary was totally unprepared and told the counselee to "get out of my office and never come back!" Later, through books and talks with fellow counselors, Gary learned the anxiety actually had come from inside, not from what the counselee had said. He'd blown up because he wasn't comfortable talking about homosexuality openly with another man. Gary eventually called the man and asked for forgiveness. Only then was Gary able to deal with the sexual problems of others.

From this background, Gary was prepared emotionally when Jan made his pass and explained to him he was confusing *phila* (friendship) and *eros* (sexual) love. Gary also could see that such a proposition probably indicated Jan's trust, or that he was testing Gary's ability to deal with the subject.

Take a Sexual History

In the third session we sought the nature of Jan's sexual relationships through taking a sexual history. In taking a sexual history, we want to discover how the client found out about sex and what his childhood experiences with it were. How did he learn about boy-girl anatomy? What did he know about his parents' marital relationship? What have been his experiences with sex? How satisfying have they been? How many partners has he had? Have there been any dysfunctions? Questions such as these are hard to ask for most people — and difficult to answer for the counselee — but they supply vital information.

Many times the person has never talked about sex with anyone else and finds such conversations embarrassing. Such was the case with Jan. Although he'd been married and had been actively homosexual for years, his knowledge of sex was limited, and he could hardly look at us when we got specific in our discussions. He was shocked that Christians would actually speak openly about such things as masturbation and oral sex. In fact, Jan, as most sexual addicts, saw sex as being dirty and un-Christian.

Because Jan had been a practicing homosexual for over twenty years, his was a long, detailed history. Although sexually involved with men in fantasy since a young child, his first actual physical encounter occurred at a Christian college when a trusted, older male teacher, Walt, led him into a caring, emotional relationship that included sex. This was a powerful experience for two reasons: Jan enjoyed the act itself, and he felt acceptance from this father-like figure. He had, he felt, at long last been accepted just as he was.

Although at the time Jan was "happily" married to a committed Christian woman and had a reasonable sexual relationship with her, he had never before felt the love, care, and affirmation that he now received from Walt. This further reinforced and strengthened the symbolic confusion within Jan's mind and convinced him that he was a "true homosexual."

Jan didn't want to lose Walt's support in the music department, so in many ways, Jan was in bondage to the relationship. However, he soon found he wasn't Walt's only partner; several others from the music department found Walt a loving partner. Hurt and angry, Jan began to look for additional sexual relationships at school. Over a two-year period, he set up numerous one-night stands.

This filled him with conflict. He was married, yet found male sex more appealing. He was studying to be a minister of music, yet afraid of God and panic-stricken at the thought of leading worship. He professed to believe in a strict code of morality, yet he was involved continually in acts that caused him enormous guilt and shame.

Jan tried to stop many times. In fact, he had discussed his dilemma with Walt and the other gay students. In general, they hated their lifestyle but felt helpless to do anything about it. They, like Jan, believed they had been born that way and were sentenced to a life of misery.

Jan had asked for help from visiting evangelists on several occasions because he knew what he shared would leave town with them. One evangelist told Jan sodomites would burn in hell and that if he had his way, all such perverts would be stoned. Another man told Jan that he, too, was gay, and they commiserated by having sex. A third cast out demons and told Jan, "To keep your healing, you have to have faith." Jan evidently didn't.

Finding no help, Jan stopped asking. Finding no understanding and compassion (except from other gays), he stayed within the gay community, which reinforced his beliefs and behaviors. Finding no power to change, he developed cynicism toward God, the church, and the Bible that promised a new life. Finding no faith, no hope, no love, he developed a settled hopelessness that turned into a callous disregard for Christian morals and bitterness toward conservative Christians and their "idealistic, naive faith."

However, because the wages of sin have not changed over the centuries, in time things caught up with Jan. He cruised one department store john too many and got arrested on a police sweep. Wanda, Jan's wife, posted bail, so his secret life came into the light. She had feared for Jan for a long time but was trying to protect him from the pain of being confronted. Fortunately, the police weren't as interested in protection, and Jan began to get help.

All this came out over several sessions dealing with sexual history. It wasn't a pretty picture, but it needed to be uncovered.

Connect History with Present Activities

In order to heal a sexual addict, we try to hold in tension two paradoxical beliefs: addictive behavior is both a disease and a choice — bondage and rebellion. Therefore, we want to get to the root of the disease — the trauma, pain, rejection, and poor parenting that the child received. In this, the child had no choice; he is in bondage to the sins of others. But we must face concurrently the choices the addict has made along the road — choices toward sin. If both sides of the problem aren't confronted, change is impossible.

While taking Jan's family history, we began to connect what happened in his family and what he was acting out unconsciously in promiscuous behavior. At the same time, we knew Jan did have a choice in determining the exact results of the trauma he received. His choices had resulted in anger toward parents and God.

The Book of Hebrews says, "Be careful lest any of you fail to obtain the grace of God whereby a root of bitterness will spring up and defile many people." Jan had failed to apply God's grace to himself, his siblings, and his parents. As a result, he had developed numerous roots of bitterness.

Jan didn't want to accept responsibility for his sexual behavior. "My father neglected me, and Mom was overprotective," he protested. "It's not my fault." Although it's true he was reared in an imperfect world, we taught Jan that his only hope for healing lay in forgiving his family and in seeking forgiveness himself.

When Jan learned the distance of his father mattered less than his childhood judgments of that father, he was able to confess his sin of judgmentalism, receive cleansing from the Lord, and then forgive his dad. Jan's feelings changed toward his family after his confession and forgiveness.

With the pattern of mutual rejection with his 80-year-old father broken, Jan's relationship with other men improved. Whereas being out of fellowship with his father had resulted in sexualizing the friendship of other men, being in relationship with Dad now allowed Jan to be a friend to men in a healthy way. He was deeply struck by the change: "It's amazing! I can have friends without getting sexual."

As we continued to work with Jan, he began to see places where he went wrong. He gradually understood that he was not hopelessly homosexual, but that deficiencies in personality and lack of affirmation had caused his behavior. He began to see the roots of his symbolic confusion and how these drove him to act out sexually. Best, he started to understand that it was only through a personal relationship with Jesus Christ and fellowship within the body of believers that he could know true love.

Break Patterns of Behavior

Though Jan had been arrested, confronted by the church and family, and was in counseling, he still was tempted by homosexual activity. He tried to stop but seemed unable to do so completely. A breakthrough occurred, however, when Jan came to see us right after a sexual experience, and we examined the events that led up to it.

Jan related that on Sunday he'd been criticized for the worship music. On Tuesday, he and Wanda had been badly defeated in tennis. On Wednesday, Wanda had criticized his discipline of the children.

In rapid succession, Jan had faced crises in his professional, social, and family life. On Thursday, he went looking for a sex partner. Perceived rejection led Jan to feel depressed, and his drug of choice for depression was sex with a man. The habits of many years were hard to break.

Early in the session, Jan said, "I went into the department store rest room and was tempted." For the next hour and a half, we helped Jan diagnose the disappointing experiences earlier in the week that led him to the department store. We look for patterns in the events preceding a sexual temptation, since real conversion depends upon changing a person's response to perceived rejection. Resisting temptation really means resisting the feelings of condemnation that cause a person to seek sexual relief. Had we not helped Jan renew his mind and emotions around the issue of rejection, in his heart he could not have repented of sexual sin. He may have been able to stop sex physically, but not mentally.

Once he began to see this pattern, progress followed. Weeks and months would go by without a sexual fall. Occasionally, Jan would fail to deal with stress and revert back to the old patterns of using sex as a drug.

When those falls occurred, we found it was his old, unrenewed belief system causing the failure. A sexual addict's belief system is filled with negative, self-rejecting thoughts. In addition, many addicts are performance oriented and live lives full of shoulds and oughts. Their constant failure to achieve irrationally high performance goals reinforces the negative self-talk and low self-esteem. Because of this, we worked to build the new Jan.

Correct False Beliefs

One continuing struggle we faced was Jan's negative view of God the Father. He couldn't trust God to meet his needs, because he projected the failures of his earthly father onto the Heavenly Father. Over and over we washed Jan's mind with the truth of Scripture in order to overcome the lies of his irrational belief system.

We gave Jan, as we do all our counselees, tools to assist him in analyzing his behavior through understanding his belief system. We showed him the ABCDs of his emotions: that Activating Events (A) are interpreted by his Belief System (B), causing Consequential Feelings (C) in him, which result in Decisive Behavior (D). We have no control over Activating Events, and Consequential Feelings are caused by what we believe about the events. The Decisive Behavior results directly from feelings. Therefore, the place to work is the Belief System.

By hitting repeatedly on his misconceptions, over time we were able to help Jan see just how irrational his belief system was, so his mind could be renewed according to Scripture. Unfortunately, much of his irrational self-talk came from the rigid theology of his youth, and this made our task more difficult.

Another young man's experience demonstrates how the belief system affects us. For six months we hadn't been able to identify any causes of his homosexual tendencies. Then in a routine counseling session, he began to tell us about something that had happened when he was 16. He began, "As usual, my father said, 'Why are you so dumb?' " The "as usual" caught our attention. When we probed, the man told how he often had sought his father's advice and his father had given it to him, but always beginning with, "What makes you so dumb? Can't you remember anything I told you before?"

Because of these words, the young man believed he was inadequate. He'd decided, *I'm never going to be capable, to measure up.* This became a powerful belief system. Change began when he saw what the Bible had to say about him. In fact, he memorized many Scriptures that affirmed his position in Christ.

With Jan, we worked weekly for about eight months until he was able to handle stress by himself without yielding to the old temptations. After that we saw him periodically for a year. Recently Jan said not only are his temptations becoming weaker and less frequent, but he no longer yields to them. Now he can even worship God in church.

Work with Family Members

At the same time we were counseling Jan, we also worked with Wanda. Like many mates, she was a co-dependent who actually facilitated his addiction. When Jan felt temptation coming, he'd withdraw from the family. Wanda saw that as a signal for her to take over. She became bossy and smothery, just like his mother had. This reinforced the "I'm not a real man" syndrome and encouraged Jan to act out his frustration in homosexual contact.

Early in their marriage, Wanda was ignorant of the depth of

Jan's addiction, but she became addicted to taking care of him. After the arrest, she was at a loss. She tended to be angry yet continue as the super caregiver.

We taught Wanda how to communicate with Jan about her own needs and wants so she would treat Jan as an adult. Strangely, we found it harder to get Wanda to change than to help Jan. He knew his behavior was wrong, while Wanda's actions seemed good and caring.

Just as a teeter-totter operates on the principle of balance, so does a family. When Wanda was overresponsible, Jan would edge toward the end of the teeter-totter labeled "irresponsibility."

Making this particular match even more difficult to untangle was the support Wanda received for her martyr compulsions, especially after Jan's perversion became known. Wanda's advisers acted with all the competence of poor Job's "comforters." They encouraged her to be "a strong Christian wife and mother now that her husband had revealed how weak willed he really was."

Convincing her she was addicted to strength was difficult, but the notion of mutual submission slowly took root and flourished. We learned eventually that her addiction developed when she was the eldest child in an alcoholic family. She had become an expert at being a co-dependent. Although growing, Wanda has much more work yet to do than Jan.

Other Examples

We've used Jan's case to illustrate our work, but perhaps you've wondered what happened to Claire and Don.

Many women who become addicted to prostitution come from families in which they were molested as children. However, Claire revealed instead a childhood filled with rejection from both parents. Claire perceived she constantly was rejected by her father, and her mother sided with him. She was the family scapegoat, making her self-esteem negligible.

Through prayer and Scripture, we helped Claire forgive her

parents and accept God's forgiveness. This step posed few difficulties. However, helping Claire forgive herself was much more difficult. It took more than eighteen months to help Claire find her way to substantial wholeness.

Don's story is not unlike Claire's. Being the third of four sons, he also got lost in his family of origin. Because he was not athletically inclined, his father was displeased. As a result, Don had serious difficulty believing he was a real man. Despite numerous visits to prostitutes — each with the unconscious assumption that this time he would feel like a real man — it never worked. The counseling process with Don resembled that with Jan and Claire.

The particulars may differ, but the principles remain constant. We always listen carefully for the hurts and beliefs of the deep heart, for Jesus said, "Out of the broken pieces of the heart, the mouth speaks" (Luke 6:45). Once we discover trauma, roots of bitterness, or lack of forgiveness, we move in with prayer, confession, and forgiveness to bring healing and growth. Whenever we discover irrational belief systems, we work to renew the mind.

Don, Claire, and Jan were all particularly responsive clients who worked hard, did their homework, and exposed to us the deepest parts of their hearts. Many resist healing and won't work like that to change. They adopt a victim attitude that says, "*You're* supposed to heal/counsel/cure me." Such an attitude breeds certain failure, because trying to rescue a victim causes the rescuer to become the victim.

Because these clients worked hard, they were able to achieve substantial freedom from their life-long addictive thoughts and acts. And free from their addictions, they were ready to contribute to life and ministry as whole people. Seeing such results makes the admittedly difficult counseling process worth every minute.

NINE

COUNSELING THE RAPE VICTIM

For many rape victims, the pastor or priest is their last hope of understanding or sympathy.

Danny Armstrong

S

he will come to your office as most others do, by appointment. The rape took place quite some time ago, perhaps months, perhaps years. Only now has she worked up enough courage to talk about it. At first she probably will not mention the rape itself, but some of her resultant problems: a feeling of despair, inability to trust people, fear, and others. If you really listen and feed back her feelings accurately, chances are she will proceed past these presenting problems to the one she really came to talk about — her rape. Your first obligation then, is to listen. Without this crucial step, she may never reveal her true problem.

If she accepts the risk and reveals that she had been raped, you should know seven feelings common to rape victims. There are others, but these seem to be recurrent.

Common Feelings

Number one is *angry*. Rape victims are some of the most intensely angry people I have ever met. They are "mad as hell" and would kill their rapist if they knew who he was and if they could get away with it. But they are not just angry with their rapist. They are angry about people's attitudes who look upon rape as a sexual crime instead of a crime of violence. They are outraged at injustice, as rapists are set free on bonds, given light or suspended sentences, or paroled early. They are furious at having been violated personally.

Number two is *dirty*. Despite numerous bathings, the rape victim cannot feel clean, at least not for a long time. She feels contaminated and degraded. Even her right to cleanliness and hygiene has been taken away from her.

Number three is *hopeless*. One day she was happy, optimistic, productive, and future-oriented. The next day she was raped. And the day after that she lost life. She was robbed of the intangibles that make life worth living. Now she barely can see or think ahead until the next day. Next week is beyond her vision, next month is unthinkable, and next year unimaginable.

Number four is *guilty*. Few people have given her any sympathy. The unspoken prejudice is that only loose women are raped. Those with whom she has been able to talk about her rape have had a morbid curiosity about the sexual aspects. It doesn't take long for the message, whether verbal or facial, to come through — the rape victim is really not a victim but a conspirator. She quickly learns to play "If." "If" I had only installed door and window locks. "If" I had only used them. "If" I hadn't gone out that night. "If" I had left a little earlier.

Number five is *alone*. Being raped is not dinner-table conversation. You just don't talk about it. But eventually she must, so she risks it with a few friends she thought would understand. They don't, and she learns to withdraw. She feels estranged, alienated, and alone. Her whole world view has been turned upside down so that she is no longer the carefree trusting person she was. She finds it extremely difficult, if not impossible, to make new friends, and the ones she had from before are drifting away because "you've changed so much."

Number six is *afraid*. When a woman is being raped, she is sure she is going to die. Never before has the victim experienced or even imagined such violence. To say that the rape victim is afraid during the rape is a gross understatement. Terrified is more like it, but words cannot suffice. And the fear doesn't leave with the rapist. The victim is now a nearly classic paranoid, fearing everyone and everything. Sleep comes reluctantly. Life is now lived on the edge.

Number seven is *grief-stricken*. We grieve when we lose something important to us. The rape victim's loss is profound. She has lost not another loved one; she has lost her own loved one, herself. She feels less than whole. She has lost control of her life. She has lost hope. She has lost dignity and self-worth.

Approaches to Counseling

Remember that up to this point you still have not spoken. You have taken a moment to sense the rape victim's state of mind and emotions. Now it's time to respond. What should you say first?

Whatever it is, you should *make sure it's clear you are siding with her*. Probing and asking questions demonstrates conditional acceptance, a form of rejection. For many rape victims, the pastor or priest is their last hope of understanding or sympathy. Rejection here is devastating. She needs to know immediately that you are an advocate, one who will take her side, one who understands. The circumstances surrounding the rape don't make any difference. She has not come for counseling as a chief witness in the midst of a trial, but as a victim in the midst of a tragedy. The pastor or priest is God's representative, and God accepts people unconditionally.

Having sided with her, you must now try to meet her needs in terms of the feelings she is having. This can't be done in a single session, nor should it be rushed. But as time and circumstances allow, several steps may be taken. Keep in mind that she has chosen to come to the minister as a "holy person," a man or woman of God, and therefore expects insight and comfort from a spiritual perspective.

First, let her ventilate her angry feelings. Point out that anger is sometimes not only appropriate, but right. Jesus became so angry that he made a whip and physically drove the money-changers out of the temple (John 2:15–16). The Bible differentiates between anger and sin. "Be angry but do not sin . . ." wrote Paul (Eph. 4:26).

Hatred and anger go hand in hand, and the rape victim feels both. Anger, however, is more general in nature. Hatred is reserved specifically for the rapist. It is more enduring, too, outlasting the multi-directed anger by far. At some point, after rapport and spiritual maturity are present, you have an obligation to assist the victim in letting go of this hate. As long as she hates, she is still subject to the rapist's control. Her emotional and psychological energy is consumed by her hatred. Only when she can let go and volitionally forgive will she regain complete control of her life. As Jesus explained it, "Truly, truly, I say to you, everyone who commits sin is a slave to sin" (John 8:34).

Your chief instruments of cleansing are prayer, the Scriptures, and, for many, the addition of the sacraments. Like the ten lepers who felt dirty, not because of something they had done but because of something that happened to them, the rape victim needs to know that she can be cleansed and restored completely (Luke 17:11–19). Ephesians 5:25–27 fits beautifully, as Paul describes the cleansing power of Christ upon his church: "Having cleansed her by the washing of water with the word, that he might present the church to himself in splendor, without spot or wrinkle or any such thing, that she might be holy and without blemish."

Baptism and/or Communion might be meaningful experiences of cleansing for the rape victim. Baptism, of course, is an initiatory rite into the Christian community and should be so regarded. But in format, it is a ceremony of cleansing and, if appropriate, might be so used. Communion, with its elements of bread and wine representing the body and blood of Christ, is also a ceremony of cleansing. Reflect for a moment on Revelation 7:14, "These are they who have come out of the great tribulation; they have washed their robes and made them white in the blood of the Lamb."

Affirm the future by holding out the hope that a return to normal living is possible. If the victim appears open to such a message, the pastor may want to affirm that our God is a God who can make evil turn against itself, that he can make good come out of evil. "We know that in everything God works for good with those who love him . . ." (Rom. 8:28).

In addressing feelings of guilt, take a two-pronged approach. We all feel both real guilt and false guilt. False guilt is placed on a rape victim by the attitudes and comments of others. She needs to hear again of her goodness, of her worth and value. She needs to be certain that she is the victim and not the criminal.

Real guilt lurks behind the scenes of every human event, and in a cause-effect world, it is difficult not to see God involved somehow. Every rape victim can look back into her own life, as each of us can, and recall the "sins" for which we may believe God is punishing us. Two things need to be done here. One is to relieve anxieties about that real guilt. This can be done fairly straightforwardly. "If we confess our sins, he is faithful and just, and will forgive our sins and cleanse us from all unrighteousness" (1 John 1:9). The more difficult problem has to do with her view of God. Is he aloof, withdrawn, and unconcerned about the individual tragedies of our lives? Is he a stern taskmaster, a "you made your bed, now lie in it" God? Is he a harsh disciplinarian, punishing us for our sins? Or is he a loving Father who hurts when we hurt and who wants to meet our needs?

To help her work through her sense of loneliness, be not only an advocate, but a friend — someone to talk to, who will listen without an agenda, except when advice is asked for. A referral to another rape victim or a support group may be appropriate, but it should not be a way of copping out. She came to the minister to find a religious perspective. Encourage her to attend and participate at church, particularly in those activities centered on fellowship.

Encourage her to call whenever she wishes. She may need assistance in getting locks and security devices installed in her home. Pray with and for her. Encourage her to read the 23rd and 27th Psalms. "Even though I walk through the valley of the shadow of death, I fear no evil . . ." and "The Lord is my light and my salvation; whom shall I fear?" are comforting words.

Finally, her grief should be ministered to as any other grief. The ministry of presence is of value. Learn what a normal grief process is like and assist her through its phases. Granger Westberg's *Good Grief* was written with a view to those whose loved ones have died, but its table of contents reads like the rape victim's diary: "We are in a state of shock. We express emotion. We feel depressed and very lonely. We may experience physical symptoms of distress. We may become panicky. We feel a sense of guilt about the loss. We are filled with hostility and resentment. We are unable to return to usual activities. Gradually hope comes through. We struggle to affirm reality."

TEN
HELPING THE SEXUALLY ABUSED

Victims of sexual abuse will disclose their painful story to an average of nine people before anyone believes them.

MICHAEL E. PHILLIPS

My wife and I strolled along hand in hand. It wasn't often we took a break from our four kids to enjoy one another. We walked past the local movie theater, and I waved to some people I knew. This is the beauty of living in a small town: you know at least half the people you run into.

"Hey Mike, can I talk to you a minute?" a voice called from behind me. I recognized Gary's voice. Our local social worker, he attended our church, and we'd collaborated many times.

"What's up, Gary?"

"Has Steve come to talk to you?"

"No. I haven't spoken to him for weeks."

Gary paused. Internal alarm bells began sounding as I watched his tremulous expression. Obviously he wanted to say something serious but didn't know how.

"Is Steve in trouble, Gary?"

"He sure is! I mean, this is really big, Mike." My wife looked back at us a few paces behind her. Gary noticed her and nodded a greeting. Then he drew me close. "He's been charged with sexually abusing his foster daughter — ten separate incidents. He could be put away for five years."

"It can't be true," I said in disbelief. "Has anyone checked out her story? She was abused before, you know, and she could have . . . "

"He already admitted it, Mike."

Gaining Background

As my wife and I walked away from that deadening disclosure, I thought back to my first association with child sexual abuse. A woman in our church phoned me one night after supper, wanting to talk about sexual abuse. She queried me to find out all I knew on the subject. Within three minutes I had given her all I knew, and most of that was bluffing.

"Would you like to know more, Pastor?" Ah, the golden question! I'd used it in sharing the gospel. Now it worked with me.

"I guess it would be helpful to know more about sexual abuse," I admitted.

Edythe told of a meeting that Friday in the high school gym. She let me know that many members of our congregation were going to be there. The more she talked, the more my curiosity mounted: *Is something going on in our town I'm not aware of?*

I went with a single objective: find out the facts. The "facts" they covered were not easy to listen to, however. To this point, I'd locked sexual abuse in my personal Pandora's box with other distant evils: homosexuality, drug abuse, shoplifting, MTV. I reasoned that these things wouldn't go away even if I launched a crusade of Crusade proportions. But I came away from that meeting — and others with church members — accepting greater responsibility for children who have been sexually abused.

I've been a director of our community support group, CASA (Communities Against Sexual Abuse) for nearly four years. When I began, my greatest hurdle was the feeling of revulsion. In addition, because I lacked training, I felt out of place both professionally and emotionally. But thanks to caring believers, I received help in the form of necessary information and practical advice.

Perhaps my greatest shock came that night at the public meeting. We were shown a short film chronicling the history of three girls who had been sexually abused. A woman told us about the frequency of abuse in Canada (which is almost identical to the statistics for the U.S.): an estimated one out of four girls will be abused in some way before the age of 18. The figure is exactly half of that with boys.

The implications took a while to sink in. That could well mean one out of four women in *my* church had been sexually abused, one out of eight men. That was difficult to accept. But two weeks later I received some confirmation.

An older woman in our church came into my office one afternoon. "Pastor, I saw you at the sexual abuse meeting last month. Are you interested in helping people who've been hurt that way?"

"Sure, I'm here to help anyone," I replied with false bravado.

She believed my half-truth. "Good, then you can start with me."

For the next hour and a half, she poured out her hurt. She had been abused by her father, her two brothers, two boys who lived next door, and her 75-year-old grandfather. Never before had she told anyone besides her mother — who wouldn't believe her.

I was shocked, uneasy. This isn't the substance of normal conversations. And I know I'm not alone. Recently, I had a pastor tell me how uncomfortable he felt around younger abuse victims. His personal struggle was easy to understand: if he is too warm and understanding, perhaps the victim will perceive it as a come-on; if he is too distant, she won't trust him. So how do you help the victim while remaining distant enough from her situation to be objective?

I have found four axioms that can balance the concepts of empathy and objectivity:

Listen Ready to Believe

I believed the woman was telling me the truth, but the hardest part to comprehend was her mother's refusal to believe her. I later discovered victims of sexual abuse will disclose their painful story to an average of nine people before anyone believes them. The horror of this woman's painful story is that some victims never make nine attempts; they give up right away.

This is where the victim will feel the most anxiety at the onset. Unfortunately, there is usually ample reason for feeling that they will not be believed. For starters, they're usually told by the abuser that no one will believe their story. For a child who respects adults, this comes as a horrendous blow. His or her only escape from one adult's transgression is the righteous indignation of another adult. When a child becomes convinced that all adults are skeptical, it becomes difficult to make the effort to reveal the painful story.

One 12-year-old girl was abused for three years by her father. Since he was a policeman, the girl knew well that most abuse victims are not believed — her father had told the family stories of misused children and how no one had pursued their complaints. Finally, the girl had had enough, and she told her tale to a social worker. Her story was accepted as truth, and an interview was set up. Unfortunately, the social worker forgot to tell the police the abuser was an officer. When the initial person to enter the interview room was a uniformed police officer, the girl began to weep uncontrollably.

The background of the child needs to be taken into account.

Usually a child has fought through myriad helpers before finding someone who will do something concrete.

Most people assume "men of God" are interested in truth, so many victims open up to pastors after refusing to give details to others. I begin any interview with repeated assurances that they will be believed, and I continue to reinforce that principle. At the end of the first session, I tell the child I believe every word that's been said. If for some reason I can't honestly say this, I tell the child I believe he or she has been terribly hurt and the hurt can be stopped.

It helps to remain outwardly calm. If I'm visibly shocked by the language and particulars of the sexual acts described, the child will interpret that as disbelief. Because the child has heard all types of descriptive words for sex, the explanation may sound coarse and confusing. If I need clarification, I can't be afraid to ask for it.

If I'm going to help victims of sexual abuse, I need to make a rigid decision to believe anyone who discloses personal abuse. In the last five years, that resolve has not led me astray. I have yet to find one child who lied about being sexually abused. More often than not, such children would rather say nothing, for the pain of being so intimately used is like an open wound that will not heal.

There are cases of children who have made up sexual-abuse stories to get someone in trouble. Statistics tell us one in a thousand disclosures will be false. Most of these are misunderstood statements made to parents who turn frantic. The rest are usually adolescent girls, afraid they may be pregnant due to a sexual encounter with a boyfriend. But false claims are easy to check; the story will change. In addition, those who make false claims usually say the assailant was unknown to them.

Among the pre-adolescent victims, false claims are virtually nonexistent. Small children simply do not make up explicit sexual details. How can they depict something accurately without prior experience? I intervened recently for a 4-year-old whose mother was worried about abuse. The child was repeatedly drawing phallic images with accurate detail. After gentle questioning, the child revealed that her babysitter had been forcing her to have oral sex with him.

Children often come into the counseling interviews

wrapped in timidity. In such cases, a superb tool is the Anatomically Correct Doll Family. The doll's body parts are completely accurate. The idea is to give the child opportunity to choose which members of the family are going to be talked about. They pick two dolls to represent the abuse duo and manipulate the dolls to show what happened, something they could never accomplish with words.

Blow the Whistle Wisely

No one likes to talk about sexual abuse. People don't want to admit it happens in their town. But one fact brings even louder howls: the family connection. Eighty percent of all sexual abuse occurs within the family. Fathers and stepfathers are the largest offender group. Then comes other male relatives, then mothers, then baby-sitters. Only 9 percent of abusers are unknown to their victims. This ends the myth of the evil man behind the bushes wearing a trench coat.

Because of this, I must exercise great discernment. The victim and the abuser are often in the same family. In the case of Steve and his foster daughter, they went to the same church — mine! It's not unusual to want to ignore the incident, to put it out of one's mind and not stir up trouble. Even so, I must take the responsibility of informing the nonoffending parent about the details of the abuse.

It isn't easy to tell such news to an unsuspecting or a desperately collaborating parent, but I've found the best way is the direct way. I often say something like this: "Your child found it too difficult to talk with you about this subject, so I'm compelled to tell you myself. ——— is being abused sexually by your husband."

This head-on approach has two advantages. First, the shock value definitely gets the parent's attention. Second, if I begin to waffle and say, "Well, we're not really sure if it's true, but we think maybe there could be something possibly wrong . . ." then the parent will rarely act on what I say. If I come across unsure, I give the parent license to act as if nothing is happening, and that's completely counterproductive. I need to impart a sense of certainty and urgency.

Parents don't want to believe what I'm telling them. For that reason, I like to take a recording of my conversation with their child. When I first talk with a child, often I'll record, with permission, the conversation on a cassette tape. It doesn't seem to affect the child, and it helps me gain the trust of the parent. Once a parent hears the child's voice tell the awful story, denial is difficult.

Blowing the whistle in an effective way often requires courage. A young girl told me her cousin was being forced to have sex with her step-father. I informed the social worker in our town, who immediately began an investigation. However, this worker was ill trained and approached the abuser instead of the victim. He denied ever having done it. Not only did the social worker believe him without interviewing the children, she told him who had made the allegation and who reported it. This left the young girl and me in a vulnerable position.

But another frightening statistic makes it worth the risk: An abuser will violate an average of seventy victims over his lifetime. The *Vancouver Province* newspaper reported a British Columbia teacher admitted to abusing 2,800 children, recording the details in a faithfully kept journal. Therefore, to ignore even one case of abuse can lead to any number of painful events.

(Most states and provinces require that any disclosure of sexual abuse be reported to the police. There is only one exception: when the sexual actions are obviously exploration and curiosity on the part of another child. That is not considered abuse. All other cases *must* be reported.)

Support the Victim

How to help the victims? Safe, reliable information is available from good secular material, which you can probably get from local social workers. It takes a strong stomach to wade through some of the stories, but we need the perspective. There is more help, however, than is found in these resources. Pastors and churches can offer unconditional love, the kind only God can supply.

Many counselors rely on techniques to build the child's self-esteem. I find it more effective to sidestep the question of worth and show victims consistent, unconditional love. Since love is really what they have been robbed of, it is what Christian counselors can try to give back to them.

I met Yvonne for the first time when her foster parents brought her to an evening service. She literally hid behind the back pew, crawling on all fours as she chased imaginary animals. She was lost in the convalescent world of dreams and ideals, rainbows and perfect pals — a favorite retreat of an abused child. She glanced occasionally at whoever was speaking, but her attention span was limited to a fleeting flash away from the inner game she was playing. I assumed she was an introvert, afraid of personal contact.

I learned, however, to dismiss any first impressions I had of Yvonne. When we called upon those needing the elders to pray for healing, she marched to the middle of the crowd and plunked herself down. She told the assembly how her father had sexually abused her for six years and how she wanted God to clean out the "awful feeling" she had inside. The elders looked at me, half in panic and half in shock. How were they supposed to pray? We had never covered this in any of our elders' meetings.

Just then, a woman stood and approached the girl. Tenderly, she cupped Yvonne's small hands in hers. She smiled invitingly at her and softly called for the men to come closer and lay on their hands — the symbol of identification and faith. This woman's prayer was full of biblical pathos, a heartfelt cry to God on behalf of the wounded. Inwardly, I praised the Father for sending his servant at just this moment and for laying his healing hands on the girl.

Watch for Surprises

In working with abuse victims, it helps to remember that the effects of abuse are often indirect. I keep these phenomena in mind:

- *The Snow White syndrome.* Many abused children have an experience not unlike Snow White. Just as Snow White was poisoned and slept until Prince Charming came along, so the victim of sexual abuse often "sleeps" through abuse, hoping it will go away. One young girl even convinced herself it was a girl whom she disliked who was the victim. This girl willingly accompanied her father on excursions to places she knew abuse was likely to occur, hoping each time it wouldn't happen. When it did, she transferred the abuse to her enemy while retreating into her private world. For years she maintained her father was a good man. This is the case with many abuse victims.

Because of this, I make a point never to belittle the offender; it turns the victim against me. Most often, strangely enough, a love relationship still exists. Children hope the "wicked witch" (the offender) will turn out to be "Prince Charming" after all.

I try to emphasize the volitional character of forgiveness. Forgiveness can be (and often must be) a dispassionate, calculated act of the will. When God sees the sincerity of our forgiveness, he then causes the feeling to be released. I find that even preschoolers can understand what it means to forgive. The advantage Christian counselors have is that we can introduce Jesus Christ to the victim.

Somewhere in counseling I like to mention that all people are sinners, but God will never fail to be perfect. Since victims desire a Prince Charming, they are often prepared to accept the salvation and the help the Heavenly Father offers. This applies especially to adults, but it also can apply to children.

While the Snow White syndrome isn't all that uncommon, when I find a victim who seems completely withdrawn from life, or one suffering from physiological or neurotic problems, I realize something deeper and more difficult is at play. I don't hesitate referring this kind of victim to a Christian physician or psychologist.

- *The pain/pleasure element.* After working with Yvonne over two years, I found she kept mentioning how guilty she felt. Her story was similar to many I have heard since. Her father treated her as a lover and not as a daughter. He tried to convince Yvonne that she was his mistress and he was doing her a favor by teaching her about sex "the safe and secure way." He was always careful to use condoms so she wouldn't get pregnant.

Her guilt lay in the feelings she experienced during the sex. Though her mind was completely repulsed, her body did experience a degree of pleasure. As she entered puberty, the pleasure level increased. Though she knew what her father was doing had to be wrong, her body occasionally would respond. Long after her father went to jail, she felt latent feelings of remorse for the pleasure her body had felt, and that left her confused.

I carefully instructed her that our bodies are built to feel pleasure even when we don't want them to. I had to reinforce this many times, especially as she began to feel sexual urges toward classmates. I explained that sex was more than self-gratification. The Bible shows it at its best as selfless love in the marital relationship. Eventually she came to accept this as the proper definition.

A victim should never feel bad because of an automatic physical response. Nor should a victim feel abuse was deserved because of the lack of resistance. I stress the idea that no child ever should be forced to have sex with an adult. When it does happen, the adult must bear full responsibility. This is important, since most victims tend to find reasons to blame themselves.

● *The need for proper distance.* I've learned to steer away from making any long-term promises to the victim of sexual abuse. I need to make sure the victim knows my role and that I cannot be on twenty-four-hour call.

This is as much for the victim as it is for my own sanity. The victims often feel the need to cling to those who show love and affection. To compensate for the lack in the past, they often will demand too much from the counselor. One young victim of abuse phoned me an average of three to four times a day. At least once a day, she would ask me to come over to counsel her. She frequently hinted at suicide, as if my refusal would set off a regrettable but inevitable chain of events.

I finally had to tell her, "You just can't keep calling me like this. Let me tell you the reasons for your calls as I see them." I went on to tell her my understanding of *why* she was calling: a strong need for affirmation, her dependency, her fear of being rejected.

The answer to her needs was to involve her in the lives of several women in the church. I let them in on the girl's situation, after asking the girl if I could. She had told others already, so I wasn't breaking her confidence. Then I followed up to make sure she wasn't latching on to one of these women as a private counselor-on-call, as she had with me. I also encouraged the victim to join a larger group, such as a Bible study or a prayer circle. This allowed her to learn to open up to others, and it offered the church the opportunity to minister to her.

Keeping a proper distance doesn't preclude showing signs of affection or warmth. It's okay to touch or hold the abuse victim, exercising the same precautions I would with any other counselee. For younger victims, sexual abuse is not so much sexual as it is abuse. They don't think much in sexual terms. They especially crave affection that isn't sexually oriented, that doesn't offend their nascent sense of dignity. Because of this, I'm not against offering a warm hug when appropriate or communicating approval through a pat on the back.

One caution: Sexual abuse is a cyclical problem; most abusers were themselves abused as children. For this reason, I work to keep victims from positions of responsibility over small children. Since sexual abuse is a power trip, one way to regain lost control is to abuse someone else. Therefore, I try to find places where a victim can receive acceptance by peers and near peers, and I want to keep a victim out of babysitting or teaching positions.

Help the Family

The family of a sexual abuse victim feels a bitter sense of betrayal. In the case of the family whose child has been abused by a relative, the imprisoned or banished loved one is anathema! The family is expected to shun the abuser and even to be glad he is gone.

But consider the price the family must pay after a disclosure:

1. Loss of income.

2. Loss of community support. Who wants to associate with a family that allows such atrocities?

3. Loss of residence. Often through community pressure and the added dimension of repeated harassment by the abuser, a great many families find it easier to move somewhere else. In many cases the abuser is the sole wage earner, and the remaining family cannot pay the mortgage and must move.

4. Loss of respect for mother. Most abused kids blame the nonoffending parent (most often the mother). As the other adult authority figure, she is assumed to have purposely ignored the abuse. As a result, there is often an acting-out period by the victim. This may include serious problems such as alcohol and drug addiction, running away from home, prostitution, and petty thievery. Abused boys often will become violent. Fire setting is common.

So what can be done for the family? First, the mother needs loving and long-lasting support from church members. Churches may consider offering financial support, since most public agencies will not help in abuse situations.

Second, I find it important to interview the siblings. It is rare to have one victim in a family, and the siblings may need special counseling, too.

Third, in cases where the abuser is not a family member, family members often feel a great deal of resentment and anger. One temperate gentleman in our body took on a Mr.

Hyde personality when he learned of his daughter's sexual assault. This smoldered for many months. But instead of enacting revenge upon the perpetrator, he took it out on other family members. He became sullen and ornery, expecting perfection from the others, while excusing his own mistakes. God confronted him eventually during a sermon, and that week he asked forgiveness of his family. Had I been watching for this possibility beforehand, I may have been able to help that family avoid a lot of grief.

Finally, most families need to be freed of guilt. Everyone seems to bear the guilt of not aiding the victim. They often track through the events perpetually to rediscover what could have been done differently. I sat in a seminar recently, in which the speaker told of her peculiar reaction to guilt. She knew her father was abusing her younger sister, so to spare the child, she played up to her father, becoming sexually aggressive. He began to use her as well as her sister. She carried the guilt of both cases of abuse almost to the point of suicide — thirty years later.

I urge support groups for victims and families. When guided by a sympathetic pastor or lay leader, they can become a unique group in which guilt can be talked over and prayed out. It's not an easy or a quick remedy, but it works.

I read this account written by a 9-year-old girl who refused to tell anyone how she was abused:

I am not being good. I feel bad. My tummy hurts and I want to yell. I'm mad. Mad and bad. They hurt little girls. They make them mad and bad. Did the brothers ever get you? It hurts badder than my dad. When I talk about it I don't feel good. I feel bad and dirty too. I want to hurt me. Then I will feel better. Do you not like me now? You will not want to hug such a bad girl.

Sadly, we can't hug this little girl, but we'll meet others like her, others who need our hugs and our love and the best of our care. They're the victims. God's love — through us — is the answer.

ELEVEN

COUNSELING THE SEDUCTIVE FEMALE

All the safeguards in the world will not help the counselor who has not come to terms with his own sexuality.

ANDRE BUSTANOBY

S he was a very attractive woman, by my estimate about thirty-five years old. (She turned out to be a well-preserved forty-five.) I introduced myself in the waiting room and told her I would be her counselor.

"I'm Colleen," she said. Then, lowering her head slightly, she looked me intently in the eye. It was one of those looks that needed no words. I got the message, even though I don't normally attract the instant attention of women.

Colleen then fluffed her hair, pulled her sweater tightly over her well-endowed figure, and looked back at me coquettishly as if to say, "Do you like what you see?" I knew at that moment that Colleen's sexuality and my reaction to it would be a primary dynamic in the counseling to follow.

If counseling were mere advice giving, her sexuality and what I thought about it would be immaterial. But the therapeutic art of counseling is far more than advice; it's a relationship between the counselor and counselee. It deals with deep emotions. It draws both parties into an intimate bond. Sometimes sexual feelings are discussed — and legitimately so, for sexuality is an important part of life, a gift of God to be under his control.

Admittedly, this kind of encounter is fraught with danger. While some naively say that truly Christian counselors should have no problem working with members of the opposite sex, experience shows that we do. Not only do we have problems handling the counselee's sexual arousal, but we may also have difficulty controlling our own sexual feelings.

As a pastor for twelve years and a counselor in clinical practice for the last fourteen, I also know that pastors in large churches may encounter someone like Colleen as often as once a month, especially if those pastors are attractive and have charismatic personalities. And while I recognize that not all counselors are male, I will refer to them that way here, since the majority of violations of professional conduct occur with male counselors and female clients.

The Old Safety Strategies

Seminaries have long recognized the problem of sexual attraction in pastoral counseling and have advanced a number of safety strategies. Although these approaches help, they have shortcomings.

One strategy frequently recommended is *the open door*, the policy that pastors leave the study door ajar when counseling women, so someone in the outer office can monitor what's going on. The problem with this is that counselees want privacy. They won't be honest about their problems if they think someone is eavesdropping. In fact, often they don't even want other members of the church to know they're seeking counseling. If someone else has to know what's going on, the counselee prefers that person be present in the room.

What's more, the pastor who doesn't have his own sexuality under control may not make any sexual advances in his office anyway. He may instead develop a relationship with a woman in a more private setting.

Another strategy often suggested is *referral*. A counselor *should* refer a counselee to whom he is becoming sexually attracted. But too often this strategy doesn't work because the counselor isn't willing to admit to himself the extent of his attraction until it's too late. By that time he's not willing to give it up and make a referral. What's more, he may be afraid the counselee will tell another counselor about the tryst.

A third approach is *team counseling*, which may be a workable alternative if the counselor has access to trainees who are willing to team counsel for experience. But to staff a church with two fully trained, fully paid counselors does not make economic sense if the primary objective is to provide the counselor a chaperone.

Even if the counselor should have an unpaid intern or be able to afford a fully trained team member, however, the systems theory of counseling must be taken into account. This theory says that a counselee's response to two counselors will be different from her response to just one. All counselors don't make good team people, either. And then there's the question of whether the counselee will accept an intern as an equal member of a counseling team. The intern's value to the effort may be reduced by the counselee's attitude.

In defense of team counseling, an analogy sometimes is drawn to a physician's protocol with a member of the opposite sex. It's argued that a gynecologist doing a pelvic exam uses a nurse as a chaperone, likewise a plastic surgeon who does cosmetic work on the female breast.

The realities of medical practice, however, don't always make this possible or even necessary. A shortage of nursing staff may require the physician to use judgment about when a chaperone is really required. Often a busy office routine may not make it practical. The physician must determine whether rapport and a professional attitude already have been established with the patient. The age difference between the physician and the patient might also be enough to settle any question.

Even if the chaperone system should be observed rigidly, however, the counselor-counselee relationship is not an exact parallel. The presence of a chaperone in a physician's examining room doesn't change the condition of the tissue being examined. But in counseling it's another matter. The presence of a chaperone may well keep a basic problem from coming to the surface, particularly when the issue is the counselee's use or misuse of her sexuality.

Some may ask, "What's wrong with that? Aren't we trying to avoid sexual abuses in a counselor-counselee relationship?"

That *is* an important consideration, but avoiding danger is not our only goal. Our principal responsibility is to help the counselee. And if the counselee's basic problem is using her sexuality to control men, the problem must be dealt with in a setting that is most likely to yield positive results.

What Happens When We're Alone

Often a woman with this problem is not aware of it. All she knows is that she experiences disastrous sexual encounters with men without knowing why. Indeed, in a chaperoned setting the counselee may be the paragon of purity and innocence. I have seen counselees with this problem function quite differently in group therapy compared to individual therapy.

This is what was happening with Colleen. Besides seeing her in individual counseling, I also worked with her in group counseling. In individual therapy, she behaved seductively, often pressing me to tell her or show her that I found her attractive. In the group she came across as a man hater and took great pleasure in putting me down.

Her man-hating façade was a cover for how she really felt — ugly and unloved, desperately desiring to be affirmed by a man. In the group she came across as a strong, competent woman who didn't need men.

My task in counseling Colleen one-to-one was to help her see that she was trying to do with me what she did with other men. The only way she knew how to relate to men was sexually, and she always wound up being used. I had a responsibility to her not to let this happen in the counseling setting. Indeed, by keeping it from happening, I likely would be the first man who attempted to have a relationship with her on some basis other than sex.

My prayer was that this would open the door to new and successful relationships with other men as well. I knew I would be under constant pressure from her to become involved sexually. The key for me would be having my own sexuality under control and understanding that a sexual relationship with Colleen would have devastating consequences: it would destroy my marriage and my fellowship with God, and it would put me in danger of professional censure. Further, sexual involvement would do a terrible thing to this woman who had come to me for help.

All the safeguards in the world will not help the counselor who has not come to terms with his own sexuality, who does not loathe the idea of sex with a counselee, and who does not feel the terrible responsibility for helping, not hurting, that soul who comes for assistance.

As counselors, we must face two realities. First, transference is not bad. It's natural and acceptable for counselees to develop feelings of affection for the counselor. Second, no safeguards will work if we don't come to terms with our countertransference, if we allow our own affection for the counselee to go in the wrong direction and lead to improper behavior. Having come to terms with our own sexuality, however, we can establish a professional relationship with the counselee.

The Professional Solution

The sexually seductive counselee needs help. She can be helped by the counselor who understands that her seductiveness is not just a "sin problem" but evidence of being terribly unsure of herself. She doesn't feel like a whole woman, and the only way she knows how to relate to men is sexually.

She needs to learn that sexuality is not only what we do but also what we are — male and female. Our gender affects our behavior and our feelings. We all need a sense of wholeness as a man or woman, as the case may be, and not just the ability to perform sexually.

My job as a counselor is to bring the counselee to that place, so far as I am able. Colleen probably could perform quite adequately sexually. But this was the *only* way she could relate to men. I needed to help her find better alternatives.

Counselors of all schools recognize that healthy feelings of worth are supplied through the affirmation of significant others. This is basic to child development, and it continues throughout life. The parent who maintains an attitude of respect toward himself and his child raises a child who believes in his own worth and the worth of others.

Thoughtful parents affirm not only the child's worth as a person, but they also affirm boys as boys and girls as girls.

There's a parallel between the parent-child and the counselor-counselee relationship. To affirm the counselee involves affirming both personhood and gender. But — and this is crucial — gender can be affirmed in a way that acknowledges both the counselee's sexuality and biblical morality.

Affirming Gender and Godliness

Just how *does* a counselor affirm a woman's gender? By being empathic, warm (what the texts refer to as "unconditional positive regard"), and genuine.

The problem comes with the woman who stirs the sexual feelings of the counselor. With this kind of woman, there is so much attraction that countertransference takes place.

The counselor meets the counselee in the reception room, and immediately his inward reaction is a combination of "Wow!" and caution. The woman is gorgeous and extremely provocative in manner and dress. His sexual response is entirely involuntary, as is his professional response of caution.

As the session begins, the counselee unfolds her story. The counselor learns that in spite of her assets, the woman is in crisis over her identity as a woman. The counselor may respond to her unprofessionally with a stated or implied, "Baby, let me affirm your femininity." Sadly, this kind of response happens even among Christian counselors.

A second, more professional response is one of curiosity: "How is it that a woman who obviously draws all kinds of male attention should be in a crisis over her identity as a woman?" The answer to this question will not come quickly or easily. Eventually the counselee will almost always turn it around and ask the counselor, "What do *you* think of me as a woman?"

The responses can range from an inappropriate "Let me show you, Sweetheart" to the opposite extreme: "I think it's time to make a referral." Or the counselor can do the hard work of dealing with his countertransference in a professional way. The scenario might go like this.

Counselor: "I'm surprised that a woman who is so feminine in appearance and manner should think so little of herself as a woman."

Counselee: "You find me attractive?"

This is a difficult question to avoid, but it can be answered with a clinical, rather than a seductive, "Yes, I do." The counselee is sure to explore this further, and if the counselor maintains a professional attitude, the discussion can be used therapeutically.

The counselor's candid admission of attraction makes him genuine. But he'd better be ready for the next question: "How attractive do you find me?" The implication is, *If you're sincere, you'll show me how attractive you find me. If you don't show me, you're not sincere.* This is a common ploy by women who manipulate men by sex.

But the counselor can bring the manipulation to light, without making the counselee feel condemned or endangering himself, by saying something like this: "I feel caught in a bind. I'm getting the message that if I'm really sincere about finding you attractive, I'll prove it by getting sexually intimate with you. And if I don't, it's because you really are a washout as a woman rather than because of my Christian and professional convictions. I'm wondering if you don't miss some good friendships with men because you need to have them prove that you're a sexually attractive woman. What I'm trying to say is that I'd like to be able to find you a sexually desirable woman without having to go to bed to prove it. I'd like to be something other than your bed-partner. I want to be something better: your friend."

Such a frank expression from a counselor raises an important question: Should a counselor really admit to finding a counselee attractive?

Assuming the counselor has already come to terms with his own sexuality, the answer is yes. The principle of genuineness is at stake. But genuineness does not require that we act out our feelings.

The genuineness of the counselor may be the very thing that provides a therapeutic breakthrough. If the counselee uses her sexuality to triumph over males, or if the only way she knows how to relate to males is sexually, a counselor who is both honest and professional can do her a great deal of good. His genuineness reveals that he has the normal sexual instincts of a male, but his conduct reveals that she doesn't need to use her sexuality to have a close relationship with a man.

Another situation can arise that requires some maturity and finesse: when a woman behaves seductively, but the counselor does *not* find her advances tempting. In this case, an entirely different problem presents itself. When the verbal or nonverbal "Do you find me attractive" question arises, how do you affirm the sexuality of a woman you do not find sexually attractive?

The key is to find an honest way of affirming her *femininity*. If the counselor has developed an unconditional positive regard for her, out of genuine feelings he ought to be able to tell her what he likes about her as a woman.

"One of the things I find attractive about you is your sensitivity to the inner feelings of others."

Or, "The thing I appreciate about you as a woman is your

vivaciousness." Note: the word *vivacious* is not used of lively men. It's used of lively women. The very choice of word sets her apart as a woman. What's more, a *man* has said, "I appreciate you as a woman."

Obviously, we must avoid gimmickry here. Ours must be a genuine response or we'll wind up doing more harm than good. But the principle is the same here as for the sexually attractive female: my job is to affirm her attractiveness as a woman while maintaining my moral and professional standards.

The Verbal Touch

Sometimes a counselee is affirmed as a person by a nonsexual touch or hug. But in opposite-sex counseling, isn't there a danger that touching will be invested with sexual meaning?

Some counselors believe that a counselor should never touch a client of the opposite sex. And many pastors, with good reason, feel that hugging and touching are inappropriate in a church context because it's too easily misunderstood — both by the person being touched and by others who observe it happening.

My experience, however, is that while physical touching may at times be misunderstood, the verbal touch is even more volatile — and unavoidable. If we have been doing our job with empathy, warmth, and genuineness, we have already touched the counselee in the most intimate way possible. A oneness already has been established. Having touched the counselee emotionally in the depth of her soul, where do we go with that intimacy?

A counselor doesn't have to touch a counselee physically to find sexual titillation, however. Some counselees have reported some heavy sexual conversations with other counselors, conversations I felt had nothing to do with counseling. A counselee has a right to feel angry when her head clears later and she feels she has been exploited. We have to ask ourselves continually, *Do the sexually oriented conversations have a therapeu-*

tic purpose, or are we engaging in conversational voyeurism?

We have to be totally honest with ourselves. Motive is the key. Do we touch (physically or verbally) out of sexual attraction, out of an inner desire to exploit the situation, or do we touch out of a spontaneous expression of care for that person, quite apart from gender? When you touch with sex on your mind, you set the stage for sexual exploitation, whether you touch with words or with body contact.

Direct Sexual Advances

I am not so naive as to think that a sexually seductive client will be discouraged by my determination to maintain a professional relationship. Indeed, as a counselor, I may be considered a challenge, and she may be all the more determined to seduce me.

Colleen was that kind of woman. At the end of a session in which I had made it clear that I didn't want a sexual relationship, she said, "Well, the least you can do is hug me." Before I could decide how to answer, she put her arms around me and hugged me with a full frontal hug, being sure I could feel her entire body. She then stepped back and looked at me as if to say, "Now, didn't you enjoy that?"

I took the initiative and said, "Colleen, there are friendly hugs and seductive hugs. That definitely was more than friendly."

Though she snapped at me for "rejecting" her, she made another appointment. In the next session I dealt with what happened in the previous one. Colleen wasn't happy about my reaction to her and my resistance, but she said she understood. When the session was over, she asked if she could give me a "friendly" hug. Once again, however, it was anything but friendly.

We had reached an impasse, and I didn't trust myself alone with her any longer. I told her that if I were going to be of any help to her, we would have to do something different. I wanted a female colleague of mine to come to the next session, evaluate where we were, and make some recommendations about where we should go.

Colleen was dead set against this. She said she would continue in my group, but she would not be part of a session with another counselor.

In our next group session, I understood why she wanted to stay in the group. She used it as a forum to attack me more viciously than ever. I knew she was angry and hurt that I didn't respond to her sexually, and it would be only a matter of time before the group would realize something was wrong.

Finally it happened. After several weeks of Colleen's outrageous attacks on me in the group, one woman demanded, "What is it with you, anyway? You act like a rejected lover, Colleen. What's been going on between you and Andy?"

This was the breakthrough we needed. After much hesitation, Colleen gave me permission to tell the group what had happened. In the security of the group, she was finally able to take off her mask and show that she felt like a frightened, unloved, little girl. I was then able to go on with her in the group and establish the first wholesome relationship with her that she had ever had with a man. If my first concern in counseling had been my safety, Colleen would never have tipped her hand and revealed her fundamental problem with men.

The way the group responded to Colleen's attacks points to another principle worth bearing in mind. Namely, there is no fail-safe way to protect yourself completely from allegations of impropriety, no matter how professional and careful you might be. However, because I had a consistently credible record of treating female clients properly, with respect and professionalism and genuine Christian concern, the group recognized that any problem in my relationship with Colleen would probably not be because of impropriety on my part. That kind of consistent track record is the best defense against such allegations.

Helping the seductive female is difficult, but it can be done. It requires that we control our own sexuality. We mustn't need female sexual advances to reinforce our own faltering egos.

But most of all, we must recognize that such women have needs that require a mature, nonexploitive love. It is the love of a father for a daughter, which on the one hand enforces a taboo on sexual activity and yet on the other hand affirms her as a woman.

When we offer that kind of love, tremendous healing can take place.

TWELVE

LOVINGLY LEVELING WITH LIVE-INS

Most people — even the unchurched and those living together — still go to a church for marriage. How we deal with them makes a powerful statement about the church's view of sex and marriage, and a memorable testimony for Christ.

GREGORY D. STOVER

Sunday morning worship was over. I was standing in the tiled corridor near the entrance to our church, chatting with the few people who still lingered. Suddenly Elaine, a woman in her mid-twenties and a member of our church, bounced up to me with a look of joy.

"Pastor, guess what!" she blurted out. "Keith and I are living together!"

Mouths dropped. The church corridor didn't seem the place to deal with such an issue, so I urged Elaine to join me in my study to discuss her situation.

Keith and Elaine are one example of a rapidly growing phenomenon confronting the church. In 1970 approximately 523,000 couples in the United States were living together out of wedlock. By 1978 this figure had more than doubled. Recent studies indicate today as many as ten million couples are living together outside the bond of marriage.

I know I can't casually glance the other way, giving thanks that such immorality takes place only "out there in the world." The troublesome fact is, an increasing number of persons who claim a relationship with Jesus Christ are joining the ranks of those who live together first and marry later.

Fellow pastors and I estimate one-quarter to one-half of the couples requesting marriage in our churches are already living together.

One such couple came to my office to discuss marriage. The man was quick to relate his experience of the new birth, which had taken place a few years earlier. Both had been reared with strong Christian values. Yet I learned later in the interview that this couple, in their late forties, had been living together for several months. When I asked how they could claim love for Christ while violating his commandments, the two replied that they simply had no justification and lowered their heads.

How should we respond to this growing phenomenon of live-in arrangements?

Private Conversations

Although I do all I can publicly to teach a healthy theology of sex, private conversations offer some of the best opportunities for ministry. Sometimes my conscience (I trust under the guidance of the Holy Spirit) has compelled me to confront professed believers who sought membership in the church while living together outside of marriage.

One such incident involved Ray and Diane. I had learned of their living arrangement and made an appointment to visit them. I was apprehensive. Even prayer had not loosened the knot in my stomach.

Seated facing them in their comfortable living room, I began. "I have come to talk with you about your desire to join Church of the Cross. I need to ask you to delay that step until you are married. If we can take a few minutes, I'd like to talk with you about the reasons for this request."

The tone in the room shifted predictably. Serious expressions deepened in their faces, but they indicated I should continue.

"Ray and Diane, I hope you understand it is not that I don't want you as part of the church, or that I don't like you. I am eager for you to be members."

"Thank you," Diane interjected. "We've found the church

very helpful and hope to be a part of it. But we don't really see any problem."

I continued. "The Bible affirms the goodness and beauty of sex within marriage but has clearly stated that sex outside the commitment of marriage is contrary to God's will. These are also standards of the church. Are you familiar with these teachings?"

"We're not sure our living together is really something God would condemn us for, but I can see how the church might not agree," Ray replied.

"The reason I feel I must ask you to wait for church membership is that as long as you continue to live together as you are, you're intentionally and visibly violating the command of God and the standards of the church. Your vows of membership will have more integrity if you correct your relationship before joining the church."

We continued to discuss the biblical teachings and the reasons behind them, but Ray and Diane weren't yet willing to accept that their live-in relationship was a sin. However, they conceded our need to maintain the integrity of the membership vows.

Ray and Diane later joined the church after getting married. They remained reasonably active until they moved to a new location. I'm not convinced my counsel contributed to their decision to get married, but I do believe a witness was made for Christian values.

Ministering to Needs

Confrontation needs to be coupled with compassion, however.

My wife and I have a friend who became involved in an illicit relationship. It began with occasional sexual encounters and progressed to a live-in relationship our friend hoped would end in marriage. From time to time we gently reminded her of Christian standards and encouraged her to re-examine her chosen direction.

When her male friend abruptly dumped her for another

woman, she was devastated and went through many of the emotions a person experiences in the wake of a divorce. We spent hours talking with her as she expressed her hurt, anger, and sense of betrayal. We invited her to meals, checked on her periodically, and in general attempted to be faithful friends.

In addition, we attempted to help her understand how her decision to cohabitate before marriage had complicated her situation. We encouraged her to trust God to fulfill her needs for companionship in his time and way rather than outside his will. When she expressed interest in renewing her commitment to Christ and becoming involved in the church once again, we invited her to participate with other singles in our church.

We need to minister like this to the needs of those who live together, even when their needs and difficulties arise directly from their sinful relationships. Those who are fractured through illicit relationships can hurt just as much as innocent victims.

They need caring people who can empathize with the hurt — and present Christ, our Redeemer, Comforter, and Peace.

Develop Wedding Policies

A blanket policy of marrying any who come may convey the impression that Christians have no standards, that the church exists for the convenience of the world. A policy of never marrying a couple living together may send the message that Christ is graceless and the church exists to judge the world.

In reality, the church exists to serve the Lord and be his instrument in redeeming the world. I want our marriage standards to project to live-ins the word of grace conditioned by a call to repentance. The policy should convey: "God loves you, and we, too, are concerned that you have a satisfying marriage. We will be pleased to assist you in marriage plans, but in coming to the church, you are implicitly seeking a marriage honoring to Christ and blessed by him. Therefore, before your wedding, we expect you to face your lifestyle and conform it to God's design. We stand ready to help you in any way we can."

Justin began attending our church over two years ago. Not long after, Sue and her children from a previous marriage became his regular companions at worship. It took no special insight to see they were headed for marriage. I was pleased they were determined to include worship in their life together, and I anticipated their approaching me about a wedding.

So I was doubly dismayed when news reached me that she and her children had taken up residence in his home.

Sure enough, one Sunday shortly thereafter, Justin and Sue came to my study. Justin smiled and said, "We want to be married, and we would very much like for you to do it." Inside I gulped and prayed for courage and diplomacy.

"Sue and Justin," I began, "I'd really like to take part in your wedding and your marriage, but I think we have a problem. I understand you've been living together."

They nodded.

"Are you aware of the marriage policies we've worked out and submit to in this church?" They weren't, so I explained our policy of marrying those who were living together only if they would rectify their living arrangements. Also, I spoke briefly about the biblical teachings on sex and marriage, the church's standard, and the idea that relationships the church blessed ought to be those in which the parties were attempting to live in accordance with God's design.

"So," I concluded, "I really would enjoy assisting in your marriage if we can work out this difficulty. But I'd like to give you a chance to respond. Apparently you don't feel your relationship is wrong in God's eyes."

Sue spoke first. "Well, that's not exactly right."

"No," Justin added, "I guess we really do know God doesn't approve of what we are doing. I always knew one day I'd have the piper to pay. We just sort of fell into it out of mutual need."

"We aren't trying to make excuses, just telling it like it is," Sue added. "We understand and respect your position, but can't you still do our wedding?"

"Would you be willing to make other living arrangements until your wedding?" I asked.

"Well, we might be," Sue allowed, "but we'll need to discuss it."

Wanting to empathize as much as I could with their predicament, I added, "I know this is probably inconvenient for you, but I believe in the long run it will allow you to enter your marriage knowing you have done what you could to make your relationship conform to God's will. That'll make a positive impact on your marriage."

They left. A few days later they invited me to their home and informed me that Justin had already moved from the bedroom, and they were willing to make other arrangements if a place for Justin could be found at a feasible price. I helped Justin locate a room with a man in our congregation. He made the move, and he and Sue will be married in our church soon.

Not all the couples we talk with will be willing to rearrange their living relationship. Yet I wonder whether unquestioningly accommodating the marriage plans of live-in couples has brought many to Christ or the church. When we offer our blessing on marriage at cut-rate prices, we devalue the goods and damage the testimony of Christ.

We have a vital ministry in the midst of our live-in generation: to lift up God's design for marriage and sexuality. Our task is to respond forthrightly and lovingly to those who deviate from God's design and to point all to the one who gives abundance in singleness and in marriage.

PART IV
THE WAY TO RECOVERY

As we saw from our statistical survey in the first chapter, most church leaders don't succumb to sexual temptation.

But many do. You may have. Counselees who come for help often have.

Is it the end of the world?

No. It may be the end of a part of life. But not of life itself. You can recover. You can help others recover.

Christianity is a religion characterized by words like mercy, forgiveness, and hope. If the statistics we looked at earlier about the high percentages of people who encounter sexual difficulties are any indicator, many people need help in claiming mercy, seeking forgiveness, and rekindling hope.

Louis McBurney tells how this can be accomplished. Chapter 13, "Treatment for Infidelity Fallout," details the steps that must be taken—and the ones that must not be taken.

Dean Merrill, editorial director of periodicals at Focus on the Family, and author of Second Chance (Zondervan, 1984), tells how we can help other Christians recover from big mistakes, particularly sexual ones. "After the Fiasco: Restoring Fallen Christians" is a word of hope to a fallen world.

THIRTEEN

TREATMENT FOR INFIDELITY FALLOUT

People need to believe the intense feelings of hurt and loss will be replaced by joy and peace, and even by being "in love" again.

Louis McBurney

N ot long ago a young couple was in my office working through a serious marital crisis: infidelity. A few months earlier she had discovered his involvement with another woman. She confronted him, and he confessed. They wanted to quickly move away from the pain, so he asked her forgiveness and pledged to never see the other woman again.

Her "I forgive you" was said, and life moved on. But after several months, for reasons they didn't understand, they remained confused and angry with each other. She reiterated her forgiveness, and he kept telling her everything was in the past. Somehow that wasn't enough to bring healing.

They had completed only one part of the very difficult process of reconciliation. There is more to rebuilding a relationship than just forgiving. In counseling couples facing this struggle, I find several specific steps helpful.

Exploring the Painful Alternatives

Many of the couples I see have never considered their options. They've made up their minds either to bail out or grit it out — without pausing to recognize their freedom to choose. I find it's healthy to stop and talk together about the choices.

One choice, of course, is to murmur "I'm sorry . . . I forgive you" and slide right back into familiar patterns of relating — the patterns that led to the breakdown in the first place. That doesn't seem very attractive to me, nor to most couples in crisis.

A second option is divorce. I know many Christians say divorce is not an option. I, too, am firmly committed to the permanence of marriage and always work toward following the biblical position. In counseling troubled couples, however, I've found that a hard-line, frontal assault with Scripture verses flying often only increases defensiveness and resistance, which makes couples feel trapped and less willing to work on necessary changes.

I've had better results openly dissecting the messy details of divorce, first examining the world's view of divorce as quick relief and then holding up for inspection the long-term negative aspects. Considering all the options — divorce included — exposes as a myth the unspoken notion of divorce as the easy solution. I make it clear that after the initial relief, most people face a period of grief for a year or more. It can be very severe, depending on the circumstances.

My wife and I have been walking a friend through her recent divorce. She is only beginning to come out of the depression after two years. Even now, when certain things remind her of her former husband, the flow of tears starts all over again.

Her ex-husband had developed a romantic attachment while continuing to say he loved her and was committed to their family. His sudden announcement of divorce completely surprised her. His relationship with his lover initially prevented him from feeling the grief of divorce. But his grief arrived later as he realized the loss of closeness to his sons.

Another consideration is a loss of self-esteem, a deep sense of inadequacy. Divorced people frequently begin ruminating, *What's wrong with me that I couldn't make our marriage work?*

Such damage to their self-concept will often persist into future relationships, making self-disclosure and trust more difficult.

My pastor friend Ken Bekkedahl lacks no opportunity to counsel divorcing couples. One aspect he always points out is the financial devastation of divorce. He asks the man, "Do you think you can afford to divorce? It may bankrupt you." That gets the man's attention! Then he can go over the particulars. Aside from the legal fees, which can be minimized, the expense of maintaining separate houses is only the beginning. Complications arise as children's needs skyrocket or a second mate and stepchildren strain the checkbook. Money alone may not be an adequate reason to stay married, but the debits of divorce can be a good incentive to reconsider the decision.

One other long-range consideration is the dissolution of the nuclear family. This has been deemphasized these days, but the problems for children of divorce remain stubbornly real and lasting. Their initial confusion, sense of abandonment, and grief is often broadcast in school problems, drug and alcohol abuse, depressive withdrawal, delinquent behavior, even suicide. The increased incidence of divorce among children of divorced parents uncovers their long-range deficiency in forming committed relationships. With a parent's remarriage, children frequently sense a further loss of the parent and feelings of rejection. There is also a stepped-up incidence of child abuse (particularly sexual) with stepparents.

Discipline further complicates the picture. Children quickly learn which parent they can manipulate, and both parents become more vulnerable to it. Let's face it: nobody wants to be the "bad guy," especially when the "good guy" is the former mate.

Even as adults, children of broken homes often say they wish their parents had not divorced. Their lives continue to bear the complications as graduations, weddings, holidays, children's births, and even funerals become logistic nightmares.

"Staying together for the children" has its merits. Our culture places such inflated value on personal pleasure and fulfillment that the legitimate needs of others, including children and society, have been ignored. I have known couples who stayed together for the children and bequeathed stability rather than strife, continuity rather than confusion. I have even seen such marriages return to close, mutually satisfying relationships as life goes on.

Even after the pain of infidelity, couples considering divorce, I've discovered, need to stare the potential cost in the face. I implant visions of hard realities beyond the immediate relief from tension.

Probing the Commitment to Reconcile

Realizing that divorce is a costly alternative can be a practical motivation to choose recommitment to the marriage. Join that to the unmistakable Christian position upholding the permanence of marriage, and there is little question of the preference for reconciliation.

There are two critical steps in the reconciliation process: (1) making definite the choice to reconcile and (2) communicating that recommitment clearly.

The decision to work toward oneness can be communicated in countless ways, and knowing what says it most effectively to one's spouse improves the chances of success.

One couple did this very effectively. She doubted his faithfulness since an affair; he questioned her ability to be more affirming and less critical. Recognizing these problem areas, they made it part of their recommitment to allay their partner's fears. He began to reveal his schedule and take her out with him more. Rather than chafing under her "control," he considered "checking in" his investment in the marriage. While stepping up her compliments and expressions of gratitude, she also refrained from being her usual negative self.

It was hard work for both of them, but those specific ways communicated best. This step anchors the whole process of reconciliation. If either person adopts a "you go first" attitude, reunion will falter or fail.

Often the guilty partner would prefer the whole sticky situation just disappear. I've heard some men say, "Hey, I came back. I chose to stay with you. So let's just forget it happened and get on with life. It's not such a big deal."

It is a big deal, however, and the betrayed partner critically needs to sense understanding. By listening to the hurt and showing he understands why it's there, the guilty spouse can help the healing happen.

I try to help each person experience the other's pain. I may ask the husband, "How did it feel to you when you were ignored (or criticized, or deceived) at some time in your life?" As he recalls that feeling, it is easier for him to respond in a nondefensive way to his wife's similar hurt. I may interpret for a wife how I believe her husband feels — trapped or suffocated or mistrusted — emotions he may be unable or unwilling to communicate. Many wives have commented, "You know, I never imagined he felt that way, but I can see now how he did."

Repairing Broken Trust and Esteem

An insult can assume many garbs. Some are unique to each couple, such as violating the private aspects of the relationship and sharing them with someone else. Others are more universal. Perhaps the most critical insult derives from the break in trust.

Since marriage's twin pillars are trust and faithfulness, when one partner commits adultery, the foundation is seriously shaken. The severity of the damage is affected by several factors.

One is the expectations of the spouse. A person raised in a home marked by infidelity may practically expect unfaithfulness.

Another significant variable is the length and quality of the marriage. A relationship spotted by conflict and disappointment may not find unfaithfulness the final blow. There was little trust left to be broken. After many years of deeply committed devotion, however, the shattering of trust will probably be devastating.

Similarly the nature of the adulterous relationship affects

the consequences. What was essentially a "one-night stand" that quickly ended causes less fracturing of trust than a prolonged affair with a history of deception and betrayal.

Under any circumstance, however, the breakdown in trust is a serious part of the hurt. Perhaps the first question the spouse asks is "How can I ever trust you again?" The injured mind begins to doubt and question every absence. Suspicion and disbelief move in where trust and confidence dwelt. These are natural and expected yet difficult feelings for both partners.

Rebuilding trust requires effort by both husband and wife. The offending mate must make special efforts to reaffirm faithfulness. This means telling one's spouse about activities and companions. It means restricting special expressions of affection. It means finding time to be alone together. It means being truthful and keeping commitments.

For the betrayed spouse, rebuilding trust includes accepting what the other says without expressing doubt through accusations. When doubts arise, first-person feeling statements — "I'm still having a hard time with my doubts and fears; I want to trust you, but my anxiety sometimes pushes me into mistrust" — work better than indictments like "Where have you been? You don't care if I'm alone and worried! You've been talking to her (or him) again, haven't you?" The first style can be heard with empathy. The second is sure to produce defensiveness. The first helps rebuild trust; the second confirms the mistrust.

I recently received a letter from a man who had successfully rebuilt his relationship with his wife. He said her attitude of trust helped him most. Even when he did things that might have aroused her suspicion, she didn't accuse him. He found himself wanting to keep her informed to avoid making her worry. His attitude changed from feeling threatened to feeling grateful. That reinforced her choice of showing trust. It wasn't an overnight miracle, but a steady, successful process.

The second major victim of infidelity is the self-esteem of the injured spouse, which must be taken into account in reconciliation. The fact that the unfaithful mate chose to stay has little effect on the level of insult felt. The overriding questions are: *What's wrong with me as a woman (or man) that I couldn't hold my mate? Am I inadequate as a person? Have I lost my attractiveness?*

Disclaimers aside, the fact that speaks loudest is: *My mate chose someone to replace me!*

Sadly, many extramarital affairs take place during the mid-life transition, a time of reassessment. Both men and women evidence a growing concern about aging and physical appearance. The sad truth is that the lover is often a younger and more sexually attractive female or a more successful, powerful male. Both scenarios reinforce the inner doubts about self-worth in the betrayed spouse.

Shame and embarrassment damage the self-image of both parties. Practically every betrayed spouse reports a heavy sense of embarrassment. They begin to imagine what others are saying about them and find it difficult to go out socially. They feel they are being blamed for their mate's unfaithfulness and, in fact, they may blame themselves.

Clearing the Way for Forgiveness

In these situations, the sense of guilt cries for forgiveness. Anger walks hand in hand with guilt. Not infrequently disbelief appears first, then hurt, then self-doubt and recrimination, then guilt, and finally anger. Allowing the anger to be realized and expressed may be threatening. In the wake of an affair, the marriage may seem so insecure that both partners avoid expressing anger for fear of driving the mate away completely.

The anger remains, however, and needs to be expressed. Anger, in itself, is no sin; it can be handled without destroying anyone. I try to prepare couples for positive uses of anger and reassure them that it can be worked through.

Anger often burns over the invasion of special places, music, and memories by the image of the lover. It smolders over the dulling of the joy of sexual play, the death of hopes for the future, the erosion of respect for the mate as a parent, and the sense of abandonment by God. Since any of these may be components of the hurt to be healed, I purposely explore all these areas with a couple.

Bill and Kathy were unbridled romantics whose feeling of being married depended in large part on sharing a wild romance. They sent each other cards and flowers. They played their favorite mood music. They regularly did unusual, spontaneous things like walks on the beach in the rain, or picnics in the snow.

When Bill discovered Kathy had been replicating some of their most romantic experiences with another man, he was devastated. How could he bring that romanticism back into their relationship? Yet it had been and would be a critical aspect of their oneness. Kathy understood his hurt but felt punished when he stopped doing the usual special things.

God provides an effective way of dealing with even the severest kinds of emotional injury: recognizing the damage and anger, communicating it directly to the offending person, and choosing to forgive.

Forgiveness, the essential foundation, needs to be understood in spiritual, emotional, and physical terms. Spiritually, we are commanded to forgive so that we may be forgiven. We grow cold in an unhealthy climate of stubbornly self-righteous unforgiveness.

Emotionally, forgiveness allows us to invest ourselves in the relationship. We cannot move toward intimacy without taking the risk to make that investment. Forgiveness is a choice; we decide to relinquish hurt rather than reinforce it.

Not many people grasp the physical aspects of forgiveness found in the neurochemistry of the brain. Memories are stored as permanent physical structures in our brain cells. Each time a specific area of the brain is stimulated, a particular memory is recalled. Memory traces can be retrieved by thought associations that select precise neural pathways to bring the stored memory into consciousness. When a specific memory trace is replayed repeatedly, that enhanced recording is more easily brought to awareness. We are familiar with this process in memorizing facts, going over and over some information until it is readily recalled.

The same thing happens with emotionally charged memories, whether positive or negative. When we have been hurt, the event and its associated feelings are deposited in our nerve cell computer. We can then either review that memory, rehearsing it into a vividly enhanced mental image, or we can choose not to allow its repetition, thereby relegating it to the unconscious. That mental, neurochemical choice is called forgiveness. The memory is still there, but when life stimuli bring it to mind, we choose to extinguish it rather than reinforce it.

So forgiveness is not a one-time, magical act that removes all memory and pain; it's a repetitive choice. The outcome is a freeing of brain energy and neural pathways that allows for positive thoughts and reconciling behavior.

When I explain this aspect of forgiveness, many couples find it fits their personal experience and helps them see forgiveness as a volitional act rather than a feeling. It also helps them remain hopeful when the old memory comes to mind. They begin to see forgiveness as a process rather than an instant cure.

Controlling Curiosity

The next step proves difficult for the injured spouse. It necessitates overcoming a strong natural drive — the universal curiosity about what happened. All the when, where, and hows become compelling questions, but I've discovered that hearing the answers only intensifies the feelings of rejection.

Learning the specific details creates distressing visual images of the mate with the lover, and this may destroy positive associations of the marriage. For instance, if a couple has enjoyed a private, romantic attachment to a favorite restaurant, that beautiful tradition may be shattered by knowing "they" went there together.

Questioning also tends to alienate the guilty spouse. One

man told me of his difficulty keeping quiet when his wife focused so on the other woman. She'd ask, "Well, did your girlfriend do that better than me?"

He knew he had done wrong, and he understood his wife's angry feelings, but he did not want to badmouth the other woman. Hearing her attacked not only made him angry and defensive but lowered his respect for his wife. It also retained the girlfriend on center stage.

That sort of reaction can be avoided if the injured spouse confines curiosity to sessions with a counselor.

Focusing on the Positive

A song from the forties says, "Accentuate the positive, eliminate the negative, latch on to the affirmative, and don't mess with Mr. Inbetween." How can a couple accentuate the positive in a marriage disrupted by infidelity? One way is to arouse the many positive shared experiences. Help couples remember the initial attraction they felt for each other. Have them talk about the special events they enjoyed together or recall the struggles they have come through together.

At a time like this, their thoughts are on the glaring faults. I remind them that they will live with whichever aspect of their mate they choose to emphasize. Choose the negative, and they will live with a diminished person. Accentuate the positive, and they give themselves the best possible qualities to relate to.

The positive can also be accentuated by keeping a sense of humor. The key is to laugh at one's self instead of the other person. The fine line between humor and hostility blurs easily. When ridiculing a mate begins, the fun is over!

To dispel some of the heavy gloom in counseling, I will gently share some foolish behavior of mine in a situation similar to the couple's. For instance, I tell about sometimes silently refusing to do something I had agreed to do. But my refusal to repair a screen so I wouldn't be "henpecked" let in mosquitoes that bit me as often as anyone else. Usually such ridiculous behavior touches a responsive chord, and those I'm counseling begin to see the humor in their own patterns.

I want a couple to move into the future together with optimism, to rebuild dreams and be excited that the level of oneness can be deeper than ever before. This calls for faith that even from this painful, sinful event, God's Spirit can bring good. And I have seen that happen repeatedly. People need to believe the intense feelings of hurt and loss will be replaced by joy and peace, and even by being "in love" again.

Exposing the "Me First" Fallacy

Researchers Dave and Vera Mace have found that couples intent on fulfilling one another's needs are the happiest. Conversely, when unmet needs and disappointments become the focus, the marital squabbles unleash criticism and withdrawal. The unmet needs loom as giants blocking the path to happiness.

Couples do need to communicate areas of disappointment — diplomatically — but they can't remain locked in a critical mode. Rather, each partner — this is crucial — must determinedly focus on pleasing his or her spouse, looking for ways to more effectively meet the other person's needs (Eph. 5:21). When we quit demanding our own rights and spend our time thinking about our spouse's needs, a marvelous phenomenon occurs: we begin to feel more cared for and less frustrated. The tendency toward selfishly keeping score decreases as our excitement in becoming a better mate grows.

The sin of adultery is forgivable. And while no magic will make the past disappear, pastoral help can make it dissipate. Relationships can be restored — sometimes to heights never before realized or even thought possible.

It's not easy, but neither is marriage under any circumstance.

AFTER THE FIASCO: RESTORING FALLEN CHRISTIANS

One reason we and our congregations feel uneasy about the ministry of restoration is that we have not talked very much about its possibility.

DEAN MERRILL

B

y the time 22-year-old Eva Eber showed up in the pastor's office, her life story was already book length. Born into a nominal Catholic family in Los Angeles, she had begun to respond spiritually in junior high when a school friend invited her to a Baptist camp. Soon she was singing in the church's teen music group and even doing street witnessing. Her parents, however, scorned her "turning Protestant," and during her senior year, Eva moved out of the house.

By age 19 she had landed a teacher's aide job two hundred miles away, and at church there she met a young Air Force sergeant who gave her the acceptance she craved. The very first intimacy resulted in pregnancy, and only then did the news come out that her lover was already married. They lived together until six weeks after Ryan was born; by then the sergeant had tired of Eva and was off to arrange his divorce and take up with someone else.

Eva drifted from job to job, and from bed to bed, over the next two years. "I just went crazy — all I wanted were arms to hold me through the night," she later admitted. "As long as a man was taking me out and supplying the cocaine, keeping me from loneliness, I was OK."

She eventually moved in with a mid-thirties divorced father of three. Occasionally she would drop in at church, faintly clutching for the anchor of her teen years. But then, suddenly, she decided to start anew in Chicago, where a friend would help her get settled, find a job. Things would be different there.

Within a month, she found herself in bed one night with her friend's former boyfriend. "God — just give up on me, why don't you?" she prayed in the darkness. "I'm hopeless." By the next March she literally had nowhere to live. A Christian she had met at her last job introduced her to an older woman named Eleanor Hill, who let Eva and 2-year-old Ryan stay with her temporarily. It was Eleanor who directed Eva to her pastor for help.

The Exasperaters

Ministering to people who have created their own fiascoes is not the same as reaching out to victims of external adversity. We are readily drawn to help those stricken with leukemia, overwhelmed by the birth of a handicapped child, hit by a drunken driver, made homeless by a tornado. They were going along in life minding their own business when suddenly, tragedy attacked. Our compassion and empathy are instantly aroused.

But what about the unwed mother who should have known better? What about the midlife man who is suddenly obsessed with trading in his job and marriage for a condo on a warm beach somewhere with a blonde? What about the Christian who's been indicted for embezzlement . . . the parents who were too harsh or too lenient with their children and are now reaping the whirlwind . . . the person whose intemperate remarks have ignited a raging family (or church) feud?

These people are in no way candidates for heroism. In fact, they are an embarrassment, a blot on the name of Christ. They make us uncomfortable, even exasperated at times. Our lofty ministerial principles tell us to stay calm, sympathetic, and helpful, and we try. But sometimes we cannot help fighting the internal battle that emergency room personnel confess when the ambulance rolls up with someone who has attempted suicide: *Why should I knock myself out trying to save her life when she didn't think any more of it than to do this?*

Echoes of the Past

At such moments, we must take a deep breath and remind ourselves that we work for a Boss with an odd penchant for bunglers and rebels. His store of patience goes to extravagant lengths sometimes, not because he enjoys playing the fool, but because he's been around so long he has already seen it all. He keeps saying things like "I will restore you to health and heal your wounds . . . because you are called an outcast, Zion for whom no one cares" (Jer. 30:17).

It does us good occasionally to remember parts of his track record. He called a man named Abram to a great destiny — and the fellow promptly ran off to Egypt . . . conjured up a fancy scam to protect himself, but landed his wife in Pharaoh's harem . . . got evicted from the country . . . taking along an Egyptian named Hagar, whose presence almost split his marriage.

This is the paragon of faith, "the friend of God"? All the honor and achievement for which both Jews and Christians revere Abraham came *after* his personal disaster.

God is the type to pick up a murderer named Moses, who in one angry moment torpedoes his career as Pharaoh's protégé. No one would argue that the murder was meant to be — but as a fugitive Moses learned the Sinai terrain, and it is fascinating to see God use that knowledge when it was time to lead a nation eastward.

The trail continues through David's midlife affair, to Simon Peter, whose apostleship reminds us that God has a future for people who blurt out things they don't mean. John Mark spoiled his initial chance at ministry (Acts 13:13) and yet went on to write the second gospel.

The case that stretches propriety is Jonah. When he decided to head for Tarshish, why didn't God just let him go on and have a nice vacation? Why not choose another, more obedient prophet to speak to Nineveh? One might answer, "God had to punish him. He could not let Jonah get away with ignoring a divine order." But why then the recommissioning? Hadn't Jonah "missed God's perfect will" for his life, now to settle for second best?

Hardly. In fact, he turned out to be the one shining success among the prophets. Most of the others got kicked out of town, plunged into dungeons, or at least ignored. Jonah's altar call drew half a million, "from the greatest to the least" (Jonah 3:5).

Sometimes God gets carried away with this restoration business.

The Kind of Lord We Serve

Such exhibits lead us — both ministers and counselees — to four conclusions about the nature of God.

1. *He is unshockable.* We human beings have the power to make him laugh, cry, smile, or yawn (especially) — but never gasp. He never claps his hand over his mouth and says to the angels, "Did you see *that?*" He has watched every imaginable stupidity, every twist of self-destructive behavior, every faux pas, to the point that he is beyond surprising.

2. *He is bent on restoring whenever possible.* "The steps of a man are from the Lord," David wrote in Psalm 37:23–24. "Though he fall, he shall not be cast headlong, for the Lord is the stay of his hand."

It would make little sense for him to give up on us, since the planet is populated exclusively by maladroit mortals. He could perhaps start over with a better breed elsewhere in the galaxy, but he has promised to stick with us and make the best of our case.

3. *He has more options than we think.* We are too prone to think there's only one way out of a bind, and even that one

way is too often *ex post facto* ("If she'd only done/not done such-and-such, her life could have been straightened out"). We forget that even human managers in business, if they're worth anything, can think of two or three ways to solve a problem. The successful manager takes roadblocks and hitches all in a day's work, instinctively looking for Route B, C, or D in order to keep the organization moving.

How much more our God? He is certainly as creative as a corporate division head, and more so. His alternatives for the future of broken people are rarely as limited as we imagine.

4. *He uses us in his restorative work — IF we will be involved.* The trouble is, too many of us are like the English ministerium who dismissed William Carey by saying, "Young man, if God wishes to save the heathen, he can well accomplish it without your help or ours." We assume that the divorced, the immoral, and the disgraced can make their own responses to the gospel like anyone else. After all, we're faithfully proclaiming the Word every Sunday; now it's up to them.

Unfortunately, most of them find it impossible to take the first step back. A man I interviewed for my book *Another Chance: How God Overrides Our Big Mistakes* said in the wake of his affair, "If you had asked me who in the Bible I was most like, I would probably have named Adam. I had gotten myself thrown out of the garden, with absolutely no chance of return, I thought. Now I was banished."

Such people are paralyzed by their shame. Nothing is likely to happen until the people of God break the awful silence.

One man who was ousted from his profession for an indiscretion took work as a hod carrier simply to put bread on the table. He was suddenly plunged into a drastically different world; instead of going to an office each day, he was hauling loads of concrete block up to the fifth level of a construction site. Gone was the piped-in music in the corridors; now he had to endure blaring transistors. Any girl who walked by was subject to rude remarks and whistles. Profanity shot through the air, especially from the foreman, whose primary tactics were whining and intimidation: "For————— sake, you —————, can't you do anything right? I never worked with such a bunch of ————— in all my life. . . ."

Near the end of the third week, the new employee felt he could take no more. *I'll work till break time this morning,* he told himself, *and then that's it. I'm going home.* He'd already been the butt of more than one joke when his lack of experience caused him to do something foolish. The stories were retold constantly thereafter. *I just can't handle any more of this.*

A while later, he decided to finish out the morning and then leave at lunchtime. Shortly before noon, the foreman came around with the paychecks. As he handed the man his envelope, he made his first civil comment to him in three weeks.

"Hey, there's a woman working in the front office who knows you. Says she takes care of your kids sometimes."

"Who?"

He named the woman, who sometimes helped in the nursery of the church where the man and his family worshiped. The foreman then went on with his rounds. When the hod carrier opened his envelope, he found, along with his check, a handwritten note from the payroll clerk: "When one part of the body of Christ suffers, we all suffer with it. Just wanted you to know that I'm praying for you these days."

He stared at the note, astonished at God's timing. He hadn't even known the woman worked for this company. Here at his lowest hour, she had given him the courage to go on, to push another wheelbarrow of mortar up that ramp. God had used a fellow believer to rescue his spirit just in time.

How We Help

It is only natural to assume that in pastoral ministry to the fallen, repentance comes first. The sin(s) of the past must be confronted and confessed in order to restore oneself to a holy God and release his blessings in the future.

Theologically, that is impeccable. Psychologically, it doesn't work very well. John van der Graaf and the people of Saint Mark's United Methodist Church in suburban St. Louis learned that a few years ago when they started a support group for divorced and separated people. "I'm a firm believer that people have to take responsibility for their behavior," says the pastor, "and I knew from my counseling that hard questions had to be faced somewhere along the way. But that was not the starting point, we decided. First we had to try to bind up the wounds."

They emphasized acceptance, warmth, and healing love from the first Thursday night on, moving to personal renovation only when people felt secure. No wonder their group zoomed to 200 members in a year.

The opening task in ministering to those who have made a major mistake in their lives is to *restore confidence*. It is to let them know that God just might accept them again in spite of what has transpired. It is to light the match of hope, to crack the gloom. As Paul says, "We fix our eyes not on what is seen, but on *what is unseen*. For what is seen is temporary, but what is unseen is eternal" (2 Cor. 4:18).

How do we do this? We use the powerful words of Scripture, of course. We say it with our body language, our openness, our touching. We say it through the stories of others in similar straits who have been restored. We let the person know he is *not* the all-time wretch. Others have been as low, or lower, and have rebuilt their lives before God.

Music can be a great ally in penetrating the spirit — for example, Phil Johnson's song:

He didn't bring us this far to leave us;
He didn't teach us to swim to let us drown.
He didn't build his home in us to move away;
He didn't lift us up to let us down.

On both the cognitive and emotional levels we convey the Christian theme that beyond death lies resurrection.

Only then are we ready to move to the second task: *confrontation*. The person who has erred must be carefully, sensitively brought to realize that this is not a case of "It happened to me" or "They did me in." This is a case of "I did it, didn't I? Others may have been a bad influence, but I made the crucial choices."

We must play the role of God's messenger wrestling with

Jacob by the stream, who at the critical moment asks, "What is your name?" What he is really saying is "Jacob, what is your real problem? You've blamed your father, Isaac, for his favoritism toward Esau; you've blamed your brother for his sour attitude; you've blamed your Uncle Laban for his shadiness — but down at the root of things, *who are you?* You're Jacob — the supplanter, the tricky one. Face it."

Some will rebel at this point. If we rush the question too soon, some will slip back into despair. But if we are Spirit-led, we will bring about a great awakening.

The pastor who counseled Eva Eber spent more than one session getting to some important roots: that while her parents had acted unwisely in some regards, she was carrying a cancerous resentment of them; that her churchgoing as a teenager did not guarantee that she was indeed a Christian; that her physical attractiveness and self-confidence was not enough on which to build a life. She eventually came to make an adult choice to surrender her problems, her value system, and her future to God's shaping, with the result that her lifestyle underwent a remarkable stabilization.

Once the cards are on the table, we are ready to move to the third step: *confession*. As Ecclesiastes notes, there is a time to be silent, but then comes a time to speak. Self-devastated people are often initially quiet; it hurts too much to air the sordid details. But healing cannot come without it.

After the Prodigal Son came to this confrontation in the pigpen and resolved to get up and go home, he was hit by a sobering thought: He could not just waltz in the front door and go to his bedroom. *He would have to say something.* Getting right with his father meant getting verbal.

So he planned his speech. "I will . . . say to him: Father, I have sinned against heaven and against you. I am no longer worthy . . ." (Luke 15:18 –19).

The exciting thing is that when he arrived at home and nervously began his speech (v. 21), he got only halfway through. The business about "make me like one of your hired men" was lost in the father's whooping and shouting for the robe and the ring and the fatted calf. That's the way our Father is.

An aggrieved spouse or employer may not be so enthusiastic in receiving our counselee's confession, but that does not reduce the value of the act. The point is to clear the offense, so the guilty person can dismiss it forever. If the interpersonal relationship can be restored, so much the better, but it is not mandatory.

Now — we dare not stop. We must complete the fourth task: *guiding the person back into the stream of worship and service.* If we lead people through only the first three steps, we have set them up for disappointment and possible relapse. If it becomes apparent that the forgiven person still bears a stigma in the church, all that preceded is thwarted.

It is sometimes hard for lay people — who weren't present for the in-depth counseling and didn't see the bitter tears of repentance — to swallow this. Most pastors can tell of situations in which God forgave, but the deacons wouldn't. Sometimes the attitude of the church is like a button I once saw in a tourist shop: "To err is human. To forgive is out of the question."

We must not succumb to irritation or disgust at such attitudes. People are not always being mean; sometimes they are just being cautious, fearful of condoning sin. In these situations, we must instead employ the creative end runs for which God has made himself famous. If tradition (or the by-laws) prevent divorced persons from teaching Sunday school, how about a neighborhood Bible study? If ministerial credentials have been withdrawn, what about a specialty ministry that doesn't require ordination?

A nagging fear sometimes comes along: "What if he blows it again?" The Devil loves to get us fantasizing about that. We must rise against such bullying and believe "that he who began a good work . . . will carry it on to completion until the day of Christ Jesus" (Phil. 1:6).

Does this mean instant reinstatement? Not usually. Reinstatement to the original post of responsibility? Not always.

Sometimes it is better to start again in another town, not because the person is running from unfinished business, but because it's not worth waiting fifteen years until everyone's attitude mellows. The Lord runs a big vineyard, with plenty of work to be done in all corners.

Rescue Training

One reason we and our congregations feel uneasy about the ministry of restoration is that we have not talked very much about its possibility. We have long maintained the façade that all is reasonably well and no good Christian steps very far out of line. Thus, when a spectacular crash occurs, we have no strategies on file for dealing with it.

Given the realities of our times, we must begin to lay down an ethos among the people that embraces rescue initiatives. We must preach the subject *on sunny days*, when there is no precipitating crisis. It is too late to talk of forgiveness the Sunday after the head elder's daughter turns up pregnant. People's emotions are aroused, and the hardliners will crucify us. We must teach, exhort, and explain the road back from failure in calmer times, so that the Christian community is prepared when the storm hits.

King David once puzzled over what to do after one of his wayward sons, Absalom, had created a family scandal and then run for cover. According to 2 Samuel 14, David came to a kindlier feeling for his son but couldn't quite bring himself to make the first move. What would people think? How would it look in the press? Maybe it's better to let the matter lie. . . .

The wise woman of Tekoa eventually brought him around with this insight: "God does not take away life; instead, he devises ways so that a banished person may not remain estranged from him" (v. 14).

That is our ministry today. Estranged, banished people are huddling in caves all around us. It is our duty to take the risk of guiding them gently back into the sunshine.